# THE CATHOLIC SPIRITUAL JOURNEY

# THE
# CATHOLIC
# SPIRITUAL
# JOURNEY

## RESPONDING TO TODAY'S CHALLENGES

James J. Bacik

Paulist Press
New York / Mahwah, NJ

*For Richard R. Gaillardetz*
*My good friend and treasured interlocuter who*
*often stimulates my thinking*
*on theology, politics, and sports.*
*Premier ecclesiologist who has enriched the*
*Church as chair of Catholic Studies*
*at the University of Toledo, president of the Catholic*
*Theological Society of America, and chair of the*
*Theology Department at Boston College.*
*Loving husband and father who is for his family*
*the face of the Gracious Mystery.*

# Contents

# Foreword

Across the world, all people have been affected by the COVID-19 pandemic. It is responsible for long hospitalizations, separation from loved ones, the inability to be with the dying, and death. Humanity has experienced long periods of isolation. The education of children and young adults has changed dramatically necessitating remote learning. Many adults are now working from home while attempting to address the educational needs of their children. Lost jobs and lost revenue have negatively impacted the economy and people are desperately turning to food banks and shelters for assistance. The elderly, especially those in nursing homes, are forced again and again into isolation.

The virus has mutated more than once as scientists work to create vaccines that save and protect. Each time that the virus appears to be fading, it rears its head again. Conversations over the use of vaccines and masks have caused grief and anxiety and in many cases anger and frustration even within households and among friends. COVID-19 continues to leave its mark and many fear that it will never leave us.

As Catholic Christians, how do we cope with the strain and distress that COVID-19 has caused? Is it possible to find comfort and peace in the wake of this devastating pandemic? These are the questions that undergird Father Jim Bacik's very valuable book, a perfect companion for our spiritual journey. Father Bacik is well known for his pastoral approach to theology and his deep desire to make the journey to holiness a part of every believer's life.

In this post-pandemic world, reliance upon our Catholic traditions provides both comfort and challenge in daily living. Father Bacik is skilled at presenting the richness of our faith perspective in a manner that is accessible to all. Each chapter considers an essential part of our Catholic life, the creed, the virtues, the gifts of the Spirit, the Beatitudes, and liturgical feasts and practices. He draws upon wisdom figures and spiritual mentors who offer guidance, along with contemporary individuals engaged in everyday encounters that call us to conversion and spiritual growth. Readers are invited to reflect on the practical implications of the journey of faith as they deal with daily joys and trials.

Each chapter distills the essence of Catholic belief, a refreshing return to the heart of our faith. With a realistic examination of the challenges that believers face, each chapter offers wisdom and encouragement that is anchored in what Catholics hold deeply in their hearts. Connecting our genuinely held beliefs to a practical way forward on the spiritual journey, the following pages provide graced guidance and support. Father Bacik guides us in a world that can weigh us down. He provides a path, grounded in the way of Christ, and directed toward God.

Following in the footsteps of his mentor, Father Karl Rahner, Father Bacik brings together the power and wisdom of our Catholic traditions with insights for *The Catholic Spiritual Journey.*

*—Shannon Schrein, OSF*
*Emeritus professor, Lourdes University*
*Sylvania, Ohio*

# Introduction

We are all on a spiritual journey whether we realize it or not. We seek meaning in a world filled with absurdity, purpose in a history that can seem aimless, commitment in a society that celebrates open options, depth in a one-dimensional culture, and integration in a fragmented life. Religions claim to offer guidance and inspiration for this challenging journey. Christianity provides traditional wisdom for our earthly pilgrimage that is embodied in scripture, creeds, theological reflection, liturgical feasts, and the personal witness of good people. That tradition is a living reality that needs to be renewed as new challenges and opportunities emerge. We need to retrieve this wisdom, recall it to mind, and make it available for contemporary spiritual searchers. Furthermore, changing circumstances require that the tradition be reinterpreted, understood anew, and explained in contemporary language that makes sense for Christians today. At times, the traditional wisdom needs to be refocused so that it speaks personally to those aware of new needs and concerns.

Effective efforts to retrieve, reinterpret, and refocus the Christian tradition make explicit the ways it illumines real existential concerns of ordinary Christian believers. We can find inspiration in faithful Christians who effectively appropriate important elements of the tradition that guide and inspire their spiritual journey.

This book demonstrates this dynamic interaction between traditional wisdom and contemporary experience. After describing the spiritual journey, the first chapter explores the common experience of the COVID-19 pandemic in the United States to uncover important existential concerns, such as dealing with isolation and establishing new work patterns, both of which remain problematic today. The following six chapters retrieve, reinterpret, and refocus elements of the Christian tradition so they can illumine and inspire Christians encountering new challenges and opportunities on their spiritual journey. Each of the chapters contains brief meditations on a traditional Catholic resource reinterpreted in contemporary language and refocused by personal examples and questions for reflection. For example, the second chapter begins with an excerpt from the *Catechism* and contains thirty-one meditations on the various articles of the Nicene Creed to help us develop a solid contemporary spirituality that avoids the fads and distortions common in a rapidly changing world.

The third chapter has meditations on the three theological virtues and several moral virtues. In recent decades, theologians have shown increased interest in virtue ethics as a way of dealing with the moral challenges presented by the contemporary world. Virtues, which are like a second nature inclining us to do good in diverse situations, are especially relevant today in dealing with our complex changing world.

The fourth chapter encourages meditation on the seven gifts of the Holy Spirit derived from the Book of Isaiah (11:1–2). Although not much has been written on these gifts in recent years, they are worth retrieving for guidance in coping with the complexities of the emerging world. We are in special need of wisdom to direct our spiritual journey and fortitude to overcome the obstacles presented by our polarized world.

## Introduction

The well-known eight Beatitudes treated in the fifth chapter remind us of the lofty Christian ideals we need to rise above the cynicism and indifference so prevalent today. For example, prayerful meditation on the seventh beatitude, "Blessed are the peacemakers," can strengthen us to promote reconciliation in our fractured society.

Chapter 6 presents meditations on liturgical feasts as well as secular holidays. Such celebrations, which touch our hearts and our minds, remind us that we are guided and inspired by shared traditions as we make the spiritual journey together. For example, Easter—the most important liturgical celebration of the Church year—has the remarkable power to inspire us with hope that our earthly journey has a destination: union with the risen Christ in the eternal happiness of heaven.

The seventh and final chapter features meditations on fifteen spiritual mentors who embody various aspects of the Christian tradition and serve as role models for us on our journey. They include the parents of Jesus, Mary and Joseph; theologians Thomas Aquinas and John Courtney Murray; activists Dorothy Day and Martin Luther King Jr.; and secular leaders Susan B. Anthony and John Lewis. The meditations highlight the distinctive virtues of each spiritual mentor and suggest ways we might follow their good example.

Hopefully, this book will not only offer helpful guidance for our spiritual journey today but also encourage further exploration of our rich and varied Catholic spiritual tradition.

# 1

## Spirituality and Catholic Resources

A broad understanding of spirituality can be found in the great religious traditions and continues to illumine our quest for meaning, purpose, identity, and hope. As human beings oriented to mystery, we long for love that is imperishable and knowledge that is comprehensive. We are individuals with infinite longings and finite capabilities. As social beings, we need both care to develop and companionship to flourish. Our very nature propels us on a lifelong adventure shaped by past experiences and allured by future possibilities. Spirituality retains positive resonances today. For example, among the growing number of Americans with no religious affiliations, there are many who say they are spiritual or are pursuing a spiritual quest.

In secular terms, spirituality relates to the search for *meaning* amid absurdity, *purpose* in an aimless existence, *commitment* in a society with countless options, *depth* in a one-dimensional culture, and *integration* in a fragmented life. For the monotheistic religions, spirituality calls for fidelity to the example of Abraham, our father in faith, who journeyed into the unknown strengthened and guided by God's promises. For Christians, spirituality refers to our *relationship* to the triune God: worshiping the Father, putting on the mind of Christ, and listening to the Holy Spirit. It is guided by Christ's command to love our neighbor, which includes assisting the needy and working for justice and peace in the world.

The use of the metaphor "journey" to characterize the spiritual quest is common among the religious traditions. For example, Buddhism identifies a "Noble Eightfold Path" that leads to liberation from the deep desires that cause human suffering, and Islamic spirituality draws on the journey stories in the life of the great prophet Muhammed, especially his "night journey to Jerusalem," a deep religious experience portrayed as an encounter with Moses and Jesus. The Hebrew scriptures center the history of salvation on the Exodus, the journey of God's chosen people, the Israelites, who flee their cruel fate as slaves in Egypt, wander in the desert for forty years, and finally settle in the promised land. This paradigmatic journey shapes Jewish spirituality, fostering a deep faith in a merciful God and an abiding hope amid suffering.

The New Testament portrays Jesus of Nazareth as the definitive prophet, the final fulfillment of Israel's hopes. The evangelist Matthew presents Jesus as an itinerate rabbi, a traveling teacher, who had no place to lay his head (see Matt 8:19–20). Luke structures his Gospel around a journey of Jesus from Galilee to Jerusalem, where he is apprehended and executed. In John's Gospel, the Word with God from all eternity made a grand journey from the Father to this earth, where, as the Word made flesh, he proclaimed the good news of salvation and then, through his death and resurrection and ascension, returned to the Father (see John 16:28). As Christians, we are called to follow Christ and to participate in his journey, empowered by the promise of the Holy Spirit.

# Spirituality and Catholic Resources

Throughout Christian history, saints and theologians have used the metaphor of journey to encourage and guide spiritual growth. For example, the influential eastern theologian Origen of Alexandria (d. 254) described the inner spiritual journey as moving through three interacting stages: *purgative*, in which beginners purify their motives and actions; *illuminative*, in which one becomes more attuned to the presence of God in their daily lives; and *unitive*, in which the "perfect" enjoy a close, intimate, dynamic union with Christ. In his classic work, *The Soul's Journey into God*, Bonaventure (d. 1274), a contemporary of Thomas Aquinas at the University of Paris, built on Origen's threefold path by describing an inner journey ascending to higher levels of contemplation. This journey goes from awareness of God's presence in the outer world—where we find "vestiges" of the Trinity—to awareness of God's image imprinted on our soul and operative in our spiritual senses, arriving at a mystical contemplation of the Godhead, mediated by the crucified Christ. The twentieth-century prolific author and Trappist monk, Thomas Merton (d. 1968), described the spiritual journey in terms of a lifelong process of moving from the *false* self, which tries to exist outside the reach of God's will and seeks happiness in worldly pleasures, to the *true* self, which finds happiness by doing the will of the merciful God who lives within all human beings. For Merton, our peace and fulfillment depend on a journey in which I "discover myself in discovering God. If I find Him, I will find myself, and if I find my true self I will find him."[1]

Psychologists have noted ways the image of "journey" illumines important aspects of human development. It encourages us to view our lives as a lifelong process of self-actualization; an adventure that is open to change and unexpected transitions; a joint venture with companions who support and challenge us; an

---

1. Thomas Merton, *New Seeds of Contemplation* (New York: New Directions, 2007), 34–36.

expedition that must deal with historical, societal, and cultural obstacles that threaten to impede our progress; and a pilgrimage that requires stamina, resilience, and hope to keep moving forward. We make our spiritual journey not in an abstract ideal world but in the concrete real world with its complex mix of opportunities and obstacles. Significant historical events have influenced both popular piety and theological reflection. For example, the fall of the Roman Empire weakened Christian confidence in a stable world and prompted Augustine's defense of Christianity. In the medieval period, establishment of universities and the rediscovery of Aristotle set the stage for the great theological synthesis of Thomas Aquinas that has had an enduring influence on Christian spirituality. Developments in the modern world, including scientific approaches to evolution and biblical studies, made possible a new theological paradigm, articulated by Karl Rahner, that still enables many Christians to continue their spiritual journey with integrity and honesty.

The COVID-19 pandemic that began in late 2019 impacted the lives of most Americans, causing immense physical and emotional suffering. It also prompted some people to engage in deeper self-reflection, revealing hidden anxieties and unrecognized motivations. Furthermore, studies during the pandemic have given us a better understanding of the broad range of existential concerns that influence the spiritual lives of people. The effects of the recent pandemic on Christian spirituality can be better understood in the context of previous pandemics that have also had important effects on Christian spirituality. For example, the Black Death (1346–1353) that wiped out a large portion of the European population was commonly interpreted as a punishment by God for immoral behavior. People blamed the Jews for the epidemic, which prompted a surge of anti-Semitism. It spawned the Flagellant Movement, a group of radical Christians who travelled around whipping themselves for the sins of humanity in a desperate effort to appease an angry God. Churches sponsored festivals and pilgrimages to holy places that brought large crowds close together, inadvertently spreading the plague.

The Black Death also generated renewed veneration of saints, seen as signs of hope and sources of healing. Chief among them was Saint Sebastian (d. ca. 288), usually depicted pierced with arrows, which, according to legend, did not kill him. Popular piety saw him drawing the deadly plague away from humanity and absorbing it harmlessly into his own flesh. Although popular devotion to the saints during the plague included superstitious practices, it did provide genuine hope for some believers, who saw the healing powers of Christ mediated by holy people.

The grim tale of the devastating effects of the Black Death also included stories of great heroic virtue practiced by committed lay Christians as well as vowed religious women and ordained clergy. Following the example of Christ, they provided care for the sick and dying, often at great risk to their own lives. For many, this ministry was not motivated by hope for cures but by compassion for those suffering a painful death.

The 1918 influenza pandemic, also known by the misnomer Spanish flu or as the Great Influenza epidemic, which killed millions of people worldwide and some seven hundred thousand in the United States, also had a profound effect on Christian life, which was compounded by the recent deaths of over one hundred thousand American soldiers in the First World War. In compliance with government regulations, churches closed for Sunday worship and parishioners found ways to pray together at home. Order priests involved in travelling ministries, such as Catholic Extension, were forced to suspend their outreach. There was a huge increase of interest in spiritualism that claimed to communicate with the deceased though seances and Ouija boards. Pandemics tend to produce scapegoats. With WWI in mind, some

Americans claimed that German spies deliberately introduced flu germs into the United States.

During the influenza pandemic, which lasted from the spring of 1918 to the summer of 1919, many Americans acted generously and even heroically in assisting the ill and dying. As in previous pandemics, vowed women religious were especially prominent in attending to the sick. In Philadelphia, for example, over two thousand Catholic sisters worked tirelessly staffing their own hospitals, helping out at public hospitals and caring for the sick in poor neighborhoods. Closed Catholic schools were turned into emergency care centers and were staffed by teaching sisters, who provided compassionate care to the dying despite their lack of nursing experience. Americans generally appreciated the selfless service of the sisters. The mayor of Philadelphia publicly declared he had never seen "a greater demonstration of real charity or self-sacrifice" than demonstrated by "the sisters in their nursing of the sick." The same story was repeated around the country. An opinion article in the *New York Times* praised "the quiet determined selflessness" of the sisters as a model for the entire country.[2]

The COVID-19 pandemic was first identified in December 2019, in Wuhan, China. The World Health Organization declared the outbreak a pandemic in March 2020 after it had already claimed thousands of lives worldwide. In the United States, the first known deaths occurred in February 2020, and a year later over half a million Americans had died from the virus. The virus affected most aspects of American lives. We did not have to deal with dead bodies in the streets, as Europe did during the Black Death, but many of our fellow citizens died alone in hospitals because visitation was restricted. We did not have

---

2. Quoted by Nancy Frazier O'Brien, "Sisters' Work during 1918 Flu Epidemic Seen as Model for Crisis Today," Catholic News Service, March 31, 2020, https://www.catholicnews.com.

as many acts of heroic virtue as during the 1918 influenza pandemic, but we did have large numbers of generous citizens who helped the needy in simple ways, like shopping for the elderly and bringing food to the homebound. We had essential workers doing their jobs at some personal risk and health providers working long hours with little time for rest. Modern science was able to identify the cause of the pandemic and suggested helpful practices, such as washing hands and maintaining proper social distance. Scientists produced effective vaccines in record time that gave people hope for the future.

For a time, the pandemic shut down many nonessential businesses, including restaurants, gyms, and retail stores. For the most part, churches complied with government restrictions that limited attendance at religious services. Many families buried their loved ones in ceremonies for families only. Churches did not sponsor processions or pilgrimages to appease an angry God, as frequently happened during the fourteenth-century pandemic. Most of the very sick were cared for in hospitals by doctors and nurses, though often overworked, and not by untrained volunteers, as was the case in 1918. Like previous pandemics, COVID-19 produced a group scapegoat. Here in the United States and other western countries, Asian Americans were blamed for a virus that originated in China. According to various reports, Asian Americans experienced an alarming increase in hate-related incidents during the pandemic, mostly verbal harassment but also physical assaults.

In August 2020, during the height of the pandemic, the Pew Research Center did a survey of how the virus was impacting the daily lives of Americans.[3] The summary of this study, published on March 17, 2021, indicated several existential concerns that

---

3. Amanda Barroso and Juliana Menasce Horowitz, "The Pandemic Has Highlighted Many Challenges for Mothers, but They Aren't Necessarily New," Pew Research Center, March 17, 2021, https://www.pewresearch.org.

generated mostly negative responses but also some positive reactions. These concerns are especially important because they not only reveal the challenges generated during the pandemic but also suggest the general themes of a relevant post-pandemic spirituality. Our spiritual journey must engage the real concerns of everyday life that are an enduring part of the human adventure, always shaped by the past, including the recent pandemic. In this regard, another Pew study,[4] conducted during the summer of 2020, indicated that most American believers said their faith was strengthened by the virus, not weakened, even though they were not able to attend church services regularly. A contemporary spirituality must deal with the split between spirituality and religion that may have been exacerbated by the crisis. The virtual participation in liturgy that sustained many during the pandemic could become a spiritual fad that replaces active, in-person communal worship. We need a solid contemporary theology that demonstrates the essential connection between spirituality and religion and clarifies the advantages of personal participation in the eucharistic liturgy as nourishment for the spiritual journey. In general, we need a theology that correlates the resources of the Christian tradition with the existential concerns identified by the Pew study.

# MAINTAINING PERSONAL RELATIONSHIPS

The main concern of Americans during the COVID-19 crisis had to do with personal relationships. Most reported negative

---

4. Patrick Van Kessel, Chris Baronavski, Alissa Scheller, and Aaron Smith, "In Their Own Words, Americans Describe the Struggles and Silver Linings of the COVID-19 Pandemic," Pew Research Center, March 5, 2021, https://www.pewresearch.org.

experiences: not able to visit relatives, losing contact with friends, mourning the loss of a loved one to the virus, and feeling lonely. Some felt that there was too much isolation; others had the opposite problem: too much time with family members cooped up in the same house, getting on each other's nerves, and losing a sense of personal space. At the same time, some Americans described positive experiences: spending more quality time with family members, sharing meals together, having deeper conversations, connecting with distant relatives by social media, and enjoying freedom from certain social obligations.

A contemporary spirituality can learn from these experiences and find new ways of enriching personal relationships. We are social, interdependent persons who need community life to thrive. Personal relationships are both comforting and challenging. As our resources indicate, the virtue of charity inclines us to set aside our own interests when a friend needs our help. The gift of patience enables us to deal with the foibles of our loved ones. The beatitude that lauds peacemakers calls us to forgive others and seek reconciliation. The season of Lent encourages a systematic effort to overcome selfishness and grow in love of neighbor. The great spiritual guide Dorothy Day, alluding to Dostoevsky, reminds us that improving our personal relationships is a difficult daily challenge, a "harsh and dreadful" task.

# BALANCING WORK AND LEISURE

During the pandemic, many Americans felt constrained in their leisure time activities: not able to go out for dinner or attend entertainment events, such as sports, concerts, plays, and movies. One sports fan felt especially deprived because not only was the minor league baseball season in his hometown cancelled but, for a time, there were no major league games on television. At the same time, some people learned to make good use of their extra leisure time by developing a new hobby, reading more, or learning to relax.

For many Americans, the virus had a negative impact on their work life: millions lost their jobs or had their hours cut; essential workers felt compelled to keep their jobs despite health risks; some working at home felt new strains on family relationships; and health-care providers became exhausted by the extra hours of work.

In contrast, some liked working at home instead of at their usual worksite. For example, one man reported "teleworking has been a welcome change, I enjoy the extra two hours a day I would have spent commuting. I also enjoy spending more time with my wife. I know I'm fortunate and I'm grateful." Such a positive response came mostly from college-educated persons with good-paying jobs, a blessing denied to workers with less education and lower incomes.

The life changes dictated by the pandemic can be helpful in working out a more fruitful interplay between leisure and work. Leisure is an essential component of a full human life. Healthy leisure activities can lift our spirits, expand our interests, and sharpen our awareness of God's presence in our everyday lives. As we see in the following chapters, the Nicene Creed teaches us that the Holy Spirit is the "giver of life," the source of the vitality nourished by leisure. The virtue of temperance enables us to recognize when we turn a healthy leisure activity, such as playing golf or bridge, into an idol, an ultimate concern that disrupts our spiritual journey. The gift of the Holy Spirit, named "piety," alerts us to the dimension of mystery in both our play and our work. The pure of heart are more likely to see God in their relaxed moments. Advent is a good time to cultivate a more contemplative spirit, and, as noted, the Trappist monk Thomas Merton is a wise guide for developing our true self, attentive to the deeper meaning of activities unconcerned with achievement or success.

Catholic theology grounds a solid spirituality of work as our way of cooperating with God's ongoing creative activity and of actualizing our potential and becoming a better person. This spirituality enables us to enjoy work that is creative and fulfilling and to cope with work that is tedious and depleting. Saint Joseph the Worker is a realistic model because, as a Galilean peasant, he did hard manual labor and was burdened with extra taxes imposed by the Romans occupying his country. The cardinal virtue of *justice*, strengthened by the call in the Beatitudes to seek righteousness, alerts us to the inequities in our economic system that leaves so many of our fellow citizens unemployed and living below the poverty level. Finding a healthy balance between work and leisure is a difficult challenge for our spiritual journey today. The virtue of *prudence* enables us to meet this challenge daily by making good choices about how we spend our time and energy. Blessed with this virtue, Saint Benedict of Nursia, the father of Western monasticism, advocated a balanced daily regimen of prayer and work. His moderate, sensible approach encourages us to find time each day in our busy work-dominated lives for leisure, including prayer, so that we avoid making an idol out of work and have the energy to do our required work responsibly.

# STAYING HEALTHY

During the pandemic, a small percentage of Americans found ways to improve their physical or mental health: for example, eating a healthier diet, getting more exercise, reducing stress, appreciating a simpler lifestyle, and keeping troubles in perspective. By contrast, about twice as many people reported deteriorating health, including becoming seriously ill with the virus and its ongoing complications; experiencing deep grief over the loss of loved ones, depression, suicidal thoughts, and increased stress and anxiety; gaining weight through inactivity; and becoming more reliant on drugs and alcohol.

An effective post-pandemic spirituality will emphasize that we are whole, integrated persons — inspirited bodies and embodied spirits — who must attend to our interconnected physical, mental, and emotional health. It will benefit from dialogue with other religious traditions and the behavioral sciences as well as the rich Christian tradition, including the resources in this book. For example, the Nicene Creed provides a Trinitarian framework for developing a comprehensive theology of human health. Individuals struggling with emotional problems could turn to a confidant blessed with the Spirit's gift of counsel. Practicing Christians could use the Lenten season to develop healthy habits, such as daily prayer and healthy eating patterns.

# MANAGING FINANCES

A small percentage of Americans reported financial gains during the pandemic. They saved money by not going out as often to restaurants or entertainment events. Their stock portfolios increased and some did not have to pay off student loans. For others, their unemployment and stimulus checks brought in more than the jobs they lost, and by working at home, they saved on commuting costs and by not taking an expensive vacation.

Nevertheless, almost twice as many Americans suffered financial losses due to the virus: millions lost their jobs; many could not pay their utility bills; others withdrew money from their savings to survive; some families could no longer afford to buy certain food items due to inflation; many small businesses lost money and went into debt; some couples lost large amounts of their retirement savings when their stock investments went down; many Americans expressed anxiety about their financial future.

The Christian tradition claims no special expertise on financial matters and economic systems. It does, however, provide strong incentives for assisting those in need. For example, the fifth beatitude, "Blessed are the merciful," reminds us that we have a moral obligation to treat others with compassion, to suffer with them, and to assist them in their need. Mother Teresa is a prime example of generous personal care for the needy. The Holy Spirit's gift of understanding encourages us to consider the systemic causes of the great wage and wealth inequality in our country, highlighted by the pandemic. The virtue of justice demands that society do all it can to create a more equitable situation. Martin Luther King led not only the movement to overcome racism but also the poor person's campaign for greater economic justice for all Americans.

# MAKING GOVERNMENT WORK

The final concern identified by the March 17 Pew study relates to how the government functioned during the pandemic. The responses were predominantly negative. Some expressed frustration that the administration did not act more quickly, decisively, and consistently in dealing with the crisis. Others felt the government intervened too much in response to an overhyped threat by forcing lockdowns, restricting businesses, and mandating masks. In August 2020, Americans reported very few positive comments about the administration during the COVID-19 crisis. A year later, they were more likely to praise the government for Operation Warp Speed that produced vaccines in record time and the American Rescue Plan that aided struggling families and businesses.

A contemporary spirituality must deal with the proper role of government in American society. The Christian tradition provides resources to guide this effort. The fourth beatitude, which praises those who "hunger and thirst for justice," reminds us that as Christians we are called to be passionate about the great task of creating a "more perfect union" and making democracy work more effectively for all citizens. In a healthy democracy, the state or government works with other segments of society to serve the common good. The principle of subsidiarity indicates that higher levels of government should intervene only if lower levels cannot adequately serve the needs of the people. The cardinal virtue of justice demands that citizens participate in the political life of the country, especially by voting responsibly. Committed Christian discipleship includes committed citizenship. We need the virtue of prudence to deal with our very challenging problems of political polarization that were intensified during the pandemic, when even the wearing of masks became a political issue. In working out a contemporary theology and spirituality in dialogue with political concerns, the influential Jesuit Catholic theologian John Courtney Murray (1904–1967) is a helpful guide, especially his insistence on rational argumentation as the best means of overcoming barbaric polarization and producing public policies that serve the common good.

A relevant contemporary spirituality must also respond not only to the concerns identified by the Pew study but also to long-standing and continuing problems, such as racism, climate change, sexism, and immigration policy. The Christian tradition can contribute a faith perspective, moral guidance, and personal witness to the ongoing comprehensive societal effort to make progress on these and other enduring issues. Furthermore, the post-pandemic era will produce new concerns, some predictable and others now unforeseen. It seems plausible that many people will continue to work at home and opportunities for remote work will expand, creating new challenges of managing long-term close relationships in the home. It is also possible that the pandemic will have enduring effects on young people coming of age during a time of isolation and disruption. For example, graduation ceremonies were curtailed, job opportunities limited, college experiences restricted, and marriages delayed. Early indications of increased anxiety and depression among young people may indicate long-term challenges that require the perspective and motivation provided by Christian spirituality. Commentators have noted a "secularist surge" during the pandemic, which has increased the number of Americans without a church affiliation and presents many unanswered questions. Will this movement away from religious practices continue in the years ahead? How many believers will eventually return to regular church attendance? Will interest in spirituality increase or decrease? A workable spirituality must be adaptable, ready to respond to very diverse needs as they arise in the future.

An effective and relevant spirituality is a product of a mutually enriching dialogue between existential concerns and the Christian tradition. As we have noted that dialogue can begin with common concerns that invite a Christian response. It can also be initiated, however, by the tradition that may detect important concerns unrecognized by contemporary secular culture.

The next chapter, on the Nicene Creed, provides a framework and normative teaching that can guide our efforts to develop a viable, effective post-pandemic spirituality that avoids fads and responds to contemporary challenges and opportunities. The other resources—including the theological and moral virtues; the gifts of the Spirit; the Beatitudes; celebrations, both liturgical and secular; and spiritual mentors—are designed to respond to perceived concerns and to identify new ones. For example, the virtue of *temperance* both illumines the struggle to achieve balance in our disrupted lives and suggests the value of a sustainable use of limited material goods in the future. As noted, these traditional resources are presented in a series of meditations meant to highlight their significance for a contemporary spirituality. They contain classic explanations, contemporary interpretations, concrete personal examples, and questions for reflection. They are just a small sample of the spiritual resources available in the vast, rich Christian tradition. They can, however, play a useful role in moving toward a spirituality that meets the challenges and seizes the opportunities of the newly developing world.

# 2

## The Nicene Creed

The *Catechism* teaches, "Whoever says 'I believe' says 'I pledge myself to what *we* believe.' Communion in faith needs a common language of faith, normative for all and, uniting all in the same confession of faith" (§185).

The Nicene Creed, which draws its authority from the fact that it stems from the first two ecumenical councils (325 and 381), is common to all the great churches of both East and West.

> I believe in one God, the Father almighty, maker of heaven and earth, of all things visible and invisible.
>
> I believe in one Lord Jesus Christ, the Only Begotten Son of God, born of the Father before all ages. God from God, Light from Light, true God from true God, begotten, not made, consubstantial with the Father; through him all things were made. For us men and for our salvation he came down from heaven, and by the Holy Spirit was incarnate of the Virgin Mary, and became man. For our sake he was crucified under Pontius Pilate, he suffered death and was buried, and

rose again on the third day in accordance with the Scriptures. He ascended into heaven and is seated at the right hand of the Father. He will come again in glory to judge the living and the dead and his kingdom will have no end.

I believe in the Holy Spirit, the Lord, the giver of life, who proceeds from the Father and the Son, who with the Father and the Son is adored and glorified, who has spoken through the prophets.

I believe in one, holy, catholic and apostolic Church. I confess one Baptism for the forgiveness of sins and I look forward to the resurrection of the dead and the life of the world to come.

Amen.

# ONE GOD

The Nicene Creed that we proclaim at Sunday liturgy has its origins in the work of the first ecumenical council held in 325 in the city of Nicaea and achieved its current form in 381 at the Council of Constantinople.

Since the Nicene Creed traditionally functions as a test for orthodoxy, the repeated statement, "We believe," suggests that we accept the summary statements as valid expressions of Christian teaching, as substantially correct interpretations of Christ and his teaching, and as traditional doctrines of the Church with an enduring value. This does not mean the credal propositions are exhaustive, complete, or the most relevant.

The Nicene Creed begins by reminding us that there is only one God. Like Judaism and Islam, Christianity is a monotheistic religion. As Christians, however, we hold that there are three persons in the one God—Father, Son, and Holy Spirit. Since in the modern world the word *person* means an individual conscious subject, there is the danger of interpreting the doctrine of the Trinity to mean three gods. Popular Christian piety at times seems to reflect this erroneous interpretation. The Creed, which itself has a trinitarian structure with separate articles on the Father, Son, and Spirit, reminds us that we are, first of all, monotheists — believers in *one* God. The doctrine of the Trinity does not undercut this fundamental belief but enriches it.

Authentic Christian teaching and practice reflects the truth that we are not tritheists but "trinitarian monotheists." In the liturgy, for example, we pray to the Father through Christ in the unity of the Holy Spirit. In dialogue with our Muslim friends, we can confidently assure them that we share their monotheistic belief. In our religious education programs, we should make sure that the language of three persons in one God does not suggest to young people that there are three Gods. Here, it might be helpful to talk about our own threefold experience of the one God: as the Father who creates and sustains us, as the Son who shares our humanity, and the Holy Spirit who guides us. Beginning with our own experience not only preserves belief in the one ultimately mysterious God but also encourages distinctive ways of relating — in practice and prayer — to God the Son as our brother, friend, model, savior, mediator, and intercessor, and to God the Holy Spirit as the inexhaustible source of truth, wisdom, justice, and authentic prayer.

*How can embracing trinitarian monotheism guide our spiritual journey today?*

# GOD AS CREATOR

The first article of the Nicene Creed declares that the one God, the Father Almighty, is the "maker of heaven and earth and of all that is, seen and unseen." The *Catechism of the Catholic*

*Church* has an extensive treatment of God the creator and of the created world (§§279ff.). The *Catechism* notes the very first verse of the whole Bible, "In the beginning God created the heavens and the earth" (Gen 1:1) and declares that creation is "the foundation of all God's saving plans, the beginning of the history of salvation" (§280). It also lauds the work of modern scholars who have greatly expanded our knowledge of the age (some 13 billion years) and the vastness of the universe (astronomers estimate over 100 billion galaxies each with 100 billion stars) and suggests that this "invites us to even greater admiration of the Creator" (§283) and even deeper prayers of gratitude.

Reflection on creation raises questions beyond the competence of science. For example, is the universe governed by blind chance or impersonal forces or a wise and loving Source? The first account of creation in the Book of Genesis, where God creates the whole world in six days and finds everything he made to be very good (1:31), provides a faith perspective on this question.

Although modern science prevents us from accepting the cosmology implied in this account, it is a helpful poetic myth that reveals important religious truths about God and his creation. The one God is the destiny and source of all that exists. Nothing exists without his sustaining love and power. The cosmos in all its rich variety is "charged with the grandeur of God," as the Jesuit poet Gerard Manley Hopkins put it, manifesting the glory and beauty of the Creator.

The evolving world is not merely the product of chance or blind fate but the handiwork of a God who creates everything out of wisdom and love. The material world possesses a fundamental goodness that points to the Source of all goodness. God is not a remote observer of the world but is present to it as the inner energy that sustains its existence and directs its development. The material world is not merely the seedbed for the spiritual world to be abandoned like the first stage of a rocket launch.

This positive view of the material world has many implications, especially our responsibility to care for our earth, that tiny part of the vast universe that serves as our common home.

*What concrete steps can I take to be a better steward of God's creation?*

# CREATION OF HUMAN BEINGS

The Nicene Creed teaches that God created "all that is, seen and unseen." Among all the creatures God created, human beings enjoy a special place in the divine plan. The Book of Genesis states that, after creating living creatures on the fifth day, God said, "Let us make humankind in our image, according to our likeness; and let them have dominion over the fish of the sea, and over the birds of the air, and over the cattle, and over all the wild animals of the earth....So God created humankind in his image, in the image of God he created them" (1:26–27).

Commenting on this biblical teaching, the *Catechism of the Catholic Church* notes that human beings "occupy a unique place in creation" as the only creatures "able to know and love" the Creator. We alone among all creatures are called to share, by knowledge and love, in God's own life (§§355–56). Our fundamental dignity as human beings is rooted in our personal relationship with the Creator. In this regard, the *Catechism* cites Saint Catherine of Siena, who, commenting on the dignity of all human beings, prays to the Creator: "You are taken with love for her; for by love indeed you created her, by love you have given her a being capable of tasting your eternal Good."[1]

Made in the image of God, we are not things but persons endowed with intelligence and free will. We can ask questions,

---

1. St. Catherine of Siena, "On Divine Providence," *Dialogue* 4, 13 LH, Sunday, week 19, OR.

gain knowledge, and grow in wisdom. We can make decisions that lead to personal growth, care for others, and serve the common good.

Imprinted with the divine image, all human beings are members of God's family, united in origin and destiny, sharing bonds deeper than anything that divides us. We are called to act on that fundamental truth by forming inclusive communities that welcome others and perceive diversity as an enriching blessing. This biblical anthropology, reinforced by Vatican II and refined by contemporary theology, challenges our cultural emphasis on individualism, which essentially denies the social character of human existence while encouraging people to do their own thing and pull their own strings. It also challenges behaviorist anthropologies that claim that human freedom is an illusion and that external factors decisively determine human behavior. Furthermore, it places our cultural ideal of self-actualization into a context of faith, viewing it as developing the intrinsic potential of the divine image at the center of our being. Similarly, a biblical anthropology reminds us that the self-fulfillment we seek is not found simply by achieving personal satisfaction but more radically by coming closer to God, who shares the divine life with us.

*How can I better reflect the divine image imprinted on my soul during my spiritual journey?*

# CREATION OF MALES AND FEMALES

Although the Creed does not explicitly mention the creation of the two sexes, biblical accounts of creation in Genesis do raise this issue. In the first creation story, God created human beings "male and female" (1:27). Many Christian theologians, such as Rosemary Radford Ruether and Elizabeth Johnson, have used this verse to argue for a fundamental equality between men and women, both created by God, both stamped by the divine image, and both given responsibility for all other creatures.

The second creation story in the Book of Genesis poses problems for an egalitarian anthropology. In this account, after the creation of earth and the heavens, "the LORD God formed man from the dust of the ground, and breathed into his nostrils the breath of life; and the man became a living being" (2:7). After settling the man in the garden of Eden, God saw he needed a partner. "So the LORD God caused a deep sleep to fall upon the man, and he slept; then he took one of his ribs and closed up its place with flesh. And the rib that the LORD God had taken from the man he made into a woman and brought her to the man" (2:21–22).

Throughout history, this story has been used to foster sexism, claiming women are fundamentally subordinate to men and should be submissive to them, an outlook that reflects, justifies, and perpetuates patriarchal structures that marginalize women.

Believers committed to an egalitarian anthropology must deal with the obvious sexist implications of a text that has the man created first as the very source of the woman's existence. One strategy is to ignore the second creation story and concentrate on the first with its remarkable suggestion of gender equality. Another approach proposed by some feminists is to emphasize the search for a partner. The man was not satisfied with any of the creatures that God presented to him and so God created the woman who did prove to be a true partner that pleased the man. This interpretation suggests that women are really the best of God's creation, the high point of a divine experiment to find the best partner for man.

It is interesting to reflect on the word *partner* in a culture that considered women as inferior possessions to serve the needs of men and propagate the race. A true partner, however, can form a loving relationship, enter genuine dialogue, participate in joint decisions, and foster mutual spiritual growth. This is, of course, not the literal meaning of this second creation story, but it can provide a fuller understanding of the account in a contemporary context. God created everything visible and invisible, including the beauty and wonder of two equal sexes.

*How can the Creation story help us overcome lingering sexism?*

# ONE LORD, JESUS CHRIST

The Nicene Creed presents a longer section on Christ, starting with our belief in "one Lord Jesus Christ." This phrase is found in Paul's First Letter to the Corinthians, where he counters the pagan belief in many lords by insisting that for Christians "there is…one Lord, Jesus Christ" (1 Cor 8:6). The belief in one Lord also highlights the uniqueness of Jesus who is truly the Son of God, as the Creed affirms.

In the Gospel of Luke, it was the angel Gabriel who told Mary of Nazareth, "You will conceive in your womb and bear a son, and you will name him Jesus" (Luke 1:31)—a rather common Hebrew name at the time, which means "God saves." Jesus officially received his name on the eighth day after his birth, when he was circumcised according to the Jewish law. He grew up in the small town of Nazareth where he learned and practiced his Jewish faith. Periodically, he traveled to the capital city of Jerusalem to celebrate the great Jewish feasts. During his last days on earth, he celebrated a final Passover meal with his disciples. After the death and resurrection of Jesus, his followers performed miracles in his name, "a name that is above every name" (Phil 2:9). In our liturgies, Christians address the Father through our Lord, Jesus Christ.

The word *Christ* is not a proper name but a title meaning "anointed" and expresses the belief that Jesus is the long-awaited

Hebrew Messiah. At the birth of Jesus, the angel of God announced to the shepherds: "To you is born this day in the city of David a Savior, who is the Messiah, the Lord" (Luke 2:11). When Jesus was baptized by John in the Jordan River, God anointed him "with the Holy Spirit and with power" (Acts 10:38), that he might be revealed to Israel as the Messiah. In his public life, Jesus fulfilled the mission of the Messiah by establishing the kingdom of God in the world. Jesus was cautious about being acclaimed the Messiah, because it carried political connotations, including the violent overthrow of their Roman oppressors. The evangelists counter this misconception by portraying Jesus as the Suffering Servant, who "came not to be served but to serve, and to give his life a ransom for many" (Matt 20:28). After God raised the crucified Jesus to life, Peter proclaimed the messianic kingship of Christ: "that God has made him both Lord and Messiah, this Jesus whom you crucified" (Acts 2:36).

By affirming belief in one Lord, Jesus Christ, the Creed reminds us that Jesus was a human being like us with a name, a mother, a hometown, a religious tradition, and a vocation. This, in turn, encourages us to identify with Jesus, to learn from him, and to follow his good example.

*How does belief in one Lord, Jesus Christ, help us maintain a balanced spirituality in a changing world?*

# CHRIST, THE ONLY SON OF GOD

After expressing belief "in one Lord, Jesus Christ," we proclaim Christ as "the only Son of God." The notion of sonship has a long history in the Hebrew scriptures, which speak about the Israelites as children of God, refers to their kings as Sons of God, and calls the promised Messiah "Son of God." The New Testament refers to Jesus as Son of God in several places. For example, in the Gospel of Matthew, God identifies Jesus saying, "This is my Son, the Beloved, with whom I am well pleased" at both his baptism (3:17) and his transfiguration (17:5). In the story of the Gerasene demoniac, the unclean spirit addresses Jesus as "Son of the Most High God" (Mark 5:7). In the Gospel of John, we read that the Word became flesh, and that "we have seen his glory, the glory as of a father's only son, full of grace and truth" (John 1:14). And in the Letter to the Hebrews, the author states that "Christ did not glorify himself in becoming a high priest, but was appointed by the one who said to him, 'You are my Son, today I have begotten you'" (Heb 5:5).

The Gospels vary concerning when Jesus was recognized as the Son of God. In Mark, written around AD 70, the sonship of Jesus is first proclaimed at his baptism. Matthew and Luke, written in the next decade, push that affirmation back to his birth, while John, written it in its final form about a decade later, speaks of the Son being with God from all eternity. Furthermore, the Synoptic Gospels (Mark, Matthew, and Luke) highlight the failure of the disciples to understand the true nature of their Teacher until after his resurrection. John's Gospel presents a gradual understanding of the identify of Jesus. For example, the man cured of lifelong blindness by Jesus refers to him successively as a man, a prophet, the Son of Man, and finally, as the Lord worthy of worship (John 9:1–41).

By the time the Nicene Creed was formulated in the fourth century, the Christian community had developed a deeper understanding of the relationship of Father and Son in the mystery of the Trinity, which led to a more developed understanding of Christ as truly the "only Son of God" with greater emphasis on his divinity.

Since Nicaea, the Christian community has continued to develop a deeper understanding of the inexhaustible mystery of Christ. Today, for example, we have a more informed view of the Son as the cosmic Christ, Lord of a vast, expanding, evolving universe.

The development of Christology reminds us of our responsibility to grow in our understanding of the Son of God and our commitment to him. This growth can take various forms: reflecting more on his example to guide our decisions, contemplating the gospel stories, spending more time in familiar conversation with him, and remembering that the divine Son of God is also truly human like us in all things but sin.

*What can I do to deepen my love for Christ as Son of God?*

# GOD FROM GOD, LIGHT FROM LIGHT

After calling Christ "Son of God," the Nicene Creed adds the following: "eternally begotten of the Father; God from God, Light from Light, true God from true God; begotten not made, one in being with the Father." These phrases were formulated at the Council of Nicaea in 325 as a response to what we now call the Arian heresy.

During the early centuries of Christianity, believers commonly prayed to God through Christ and celebrated baptism in the name of the Father, Son, and Holy Spirit, without much speculation about the relationship of the Father and the Son. Early in the fourth century, some theologians emphasized the unity and equality of the Father and the Son, while others defended a strict monotheism that subordinated the Son to the Father. Arius (256–336), a respected priest serving in Alexandria, popularized a subordinationist position that eventually spread throughout the Roman Empire. According to his critics, Arius taught that the Son of God was not eternal but was subordinate to God—that there was a time when he did not exist. In other words, the Son is not like the Father in essence but is a creature, the greatest of creatures, but still a creature subject to change.

The Council of Nicaea, which was called by Emperor Constantine to unify his empire divided over this theological dispute, formulated its creed to refute the Arian subordinationism and to establish norms for orthodox belief. After refusing to sign the credal statement, Arius was banished, and his writings were destroyed by order of Constantine. Regardless, Arianism spread throughout the empire and even became dominant during the fourth century.

The Nicene Creed clearly affirms Christ's eternal divinity. The Son was begotten, not made or created, as Arius claimed. He was "born of the Father before all ages" so that there was never a time when the Son did not exist, as the subordinationists taught. The creed makes a distinction between "begotten" and "created" while Arius effectively made them synonyms by interpreting "begotten" as a figurative way of saying God created the Son by an act of the divine will. The phrase "one in being with the Father," a translation of the Greek word *homoousios*, which means of the same substance or essence, served as the decisive refutation of Arianism and became the key word in the ongoing debate.

Note the limitations of this part of the Nicene Creed: the abstract language is hard to understand and is not designed to touch the heart. The English word *consubstantial* is especially troubling since it sounds so archaic. The great emphasis on Christ as true God can obscure the equally important belief that he is also true man, which makes it more difficult to identify with him. Nevertheless, the regular repetition of the orthodox statements about Christ links us with Christians, past and present, who accept him as the Lord. Such a profound sense of solidarity has special significance in today's fragmented world.

*How can belief in the divinity of Christ help us deal with cultural relativism?*

# CHRIST CAME DOWN FROM HEAVEN

After emphasizing the full divinity of Christ, the Nicene Creed states, "For us men and for our salvation, he came down from heaven." The statement reflects the teaching and imagery of the prologue to John's Gospel, which declares that the Word, who was present to God in the beginning, "became flesh and lived among us" (John 1:14). We get an image of the Son of God dwelling above us and then coming down to our earth. From the early centuries of Christianity, this "descending Christology," as it is called by theologians, has been the dominant view of the incarnation among orthodox believers. Since the middle of the twentieth century, however, scripture scholars and theologians have noted that modern science has rendered the biblical three-decker cosmology (the earth in the middle between heaven above and hell below) untenable and made the descending Christology seem mythological.

Recognizing the problem, the German Jesuit theologian Karl Rahner proposed an "ascending Christology" that provides another perspective, while safeguarding the divinity of Christ so clearly affirmed in the Nicene Creed. The Rahnerian alternative begins not with the Gospel of John but with the Synoptic Gospels that portray the efforts of the man Jesus of Nazareth to articulate his identity and mission to followers, who only gradually come to see him as Messiah and Son of God. It assumes that the fundamental dynamic of human development is created by the meeting of God's self-giving love and human receptivity. In this framework, it is possible to think of a person who is so obedient to God's will, so open to divine grace that this person is totally God-possessed, the perfect image of divine love—both truly human and truly God.

The Christian claim is that this possibility has occurred in human history in the person of Jesus of Nazareth, the crucified and risen Lord—the paradigm of fulfilled humanity and the abiding presence of the Word made flesh. Rahner's ascending Christology connects with the modern scientific view of an evolving world and safeguards the full humanity of Christ, which can be obscured by the emphasis on Christ's divinity in the Nicene Creed.

It is important to remember the limitations of both official creeds and theological explanations. These always remain partial and historically conditioned efforts to elucidate the ultimately incomprehensible mystery of God's relationship to us and our world. In this case, the Nicene Creed is a consistent and powerful witness to the divinity of Christ, while the ascending Christology safeguards his humanity.

For those understandably distressed by the phrase "for us men," the problem lies with the translation and not the original text, since both the Greek *anthropos* and the Latin *homo* are gender inclusive. The stilted translation of the Creed and of the whole Roman Missal was forced on us and the other English-speaking countries in 2011 by the Roman Curia, in violation of the directive of Vatican II that gave national hierarchies authority over liturgical translations. Despite theological limitations and translation problems, proclaiming the Creed together at Mass does join us in a common effort to affirm Christ as our Lord.

*How can I practice my faith in Christ daily?*

# CHRIST WAS BORN OF THE VIRGIN MARY

The doctrine of the incarnation affirms the historical fact that the Word of God became a human being, Jesus born of Mary, who continues as the risen Christ to join full divinity and full humanity in his person. This dogma is rooted in the New Testament: "the Word became flesh" (John 1:14); Christ "emptied himself, taking the form of a slave, being born in human likeness" (Phil 2:7); and "God sent his Son, born of a woman" (Gal 4:4).

Belief in the incarnation is the distinctive sign of authentic Christian faith. It stands against various heretical claims: Jesus was not fully human, did not have a human body capable of suffering, and did not have a human will that involved decision making. The incarnation means that the *Word became flesh* and that the *Son of God became truly human*.

The mention of Mary indicates the narrative aspect of the Creed. The incarnation is revealed in the context of a story about the covenant God made with the Israelites and the divine promise to send an offspring of the great King David as the Messiah to reign in peace forever. The incarnation is a historical event generated by God's self-giving love meeting the total receptivity of Mary, who declares, "Here am I, the servant of the Lord; let it be with me according to your word" (Luke 1:38).

After noting the birth of Jesus, the Creed says nothing about important elements of his public life: for example, his exorcisms and cures, his teaching and parables, his conflicts with the scribes and Pharisees, his reliance on prayer and celebration of the great Jewish feasts, his relationship to his family and disciples, and his care for the poor and marginalized. The next thing the Creed notes is his crucifixion under Pontius Pilate.

Some scholars say it puts the emphasis not on what Jesus did but on who he is, the Son of God worthy of our total commitment. Others say the Creed is by nature a summary and that its silence on the public life of Jesus encourages us to go back to the Gospels, eager to know more about the Jewish man born of Mary. We could also note that the master evangelizer, the Apostle Paul, brought the faith to Europe while saying very little about the public ministry of Jesus, and concentrated almost exclusively on proclaiming the death and resurrection of Christ. Perhaps the simplest explanation is that the Nicene Creed was formulated not to foster spiritual growth but to set guidelines for orthodoxy in dealing with the Arian heresy that denied the full divinity of Christ. As such, it still functions today as an interpretive framework for reflecting on the inspiring stories in the Gospels. The Jesus who cured the blind man and told the parable of the prodigal son was the Word Incarnate, the Son of God made flesh.

*How can a better understanding of the incarnation help us develop a more effective contemporary spirituality?*

# CRUCIFIED UNDER PONTIUS PILATE

After noting the birth of Jesus, the Creed moves immediately to his death: "for our sake he was crucified under Pontius Pilate." Pilate served as the governor of Judea under the emperor Tiberius from AD 26 to 36. A recently discovered stone inscription in the capital city, Caesarea, where Pilate resided, indicates that his official title was "prefect." According to the Jewish historian Josephus, Pilate was a headstrong authoritarian, who unnecessarily offended Jewish sensibilities and provoked Samaritans and Jews to riot and organize public demonstrations against him. In at least one case, he submitted to the demands of Jews, demonstrating in Caesarea, that the Roman soldiers stationed in Jerusalem no longer display images of the emperor. From Roman records, we know Pilate was called back to Rome and put on trial for cruelty and for executing individuals without a proper trial.

Pilate governed Judea using vassal kings to control the population and collect the Roman taxes. Herod Antipas oversaw Galilee where Jesus spent most of his life in the town of Nazareth. From the Gospels, we know Antipas, at the instigation of his second wife Herodias, imprisoned John the Baptist and later had him beheaded (see Mark 6:14–29). From Luke's Gospel, we know Pilate sent Jesus to Herod during his Roman trial. Secular records tell us that Herod built two major cities, Tiberias, on the western shore of the Sea of Galilee, and Sepphoris, a little less than four miles north of Nazareth. We also know that in a society with no middle class, Jesus was among the poor, living under Roman occupation.

In his masterful two-volume work *The Death of the Messiah*, the great scripture scholar Raymond Brown provides a detailed analysis of Pilate's trial of Jesus. Here are some of his conclusions. In conducting the trial, Pilate was weak and vacillating but did not violate any Roman laws. He took seriously the fundamental charge that Jesus claimed to be "king of the Jews" and ignored the religious charges. Three times he solemnly declared the innocence of Jesus, as attested in the Gospels of both Luke and John.

The Gospels do not give a uniform portrayal of Pilate. In John, he is indecisive and violates judicial norms by giving in to pressure; in Mark, he is not as malevolent as the chief priests but is a poor representative of Roman justice; and in Matthew, Pilate is a tortured judge who is forced to condemn Jesus against his better judgment and who then tries to avoid responsibility for his misconduct by symbolically washing his hands. Luke's Pilate knows Jesus is innocent and is looking for a way out by sending him to Herod Antipas. Fearing the chief priests and the crowds, Pilate tries to placate them by scourging Jesus, but when this fails, he condemns him to death even though he is innocent. After noting that the Gospels say the crowds preferred Barabbas over Jesus, Brown concludes that "in all the Gospels the mass opposition to him [Jesus] is what ultimately forces Pilate to accede to the crucifixion."

*How can the Roman complicity in the death of Jesus help us challenge systemic evil in our world today?*

# FOR OUR SAKE

Christ was crucified "for our sake." The implication is that we need help, that something is essentially wrong with the human condition requiring attention, and that the human family suffers from a wound that cries out for healing. The Christian tradition calls this wound "original sin," which is a universal and permanent flaw in human nature affecting all people in all cultures throughout history. In the Book of Genesis, we have the story of Adam and Eve, living harmoniously in a beautiful garden, who disobey God's command and bring pain, suffering, and death into the world. In the story, the devil convinces Eve that if she and Adam eat the forbidden fruit of the tree in the middle of the garden, they will be like God and know all things. Although this influential myth cannot be squared with the scientific understanding of the primitive beginnings of the human species, its essential teaching that human nature is wounded because of sin remains a fundamental Christian truth. Original sin compounded by our personal sins continues to disrupt human existence.

The teaching that Christ died and rose for our salvation is expressed in the New Testament in various ways. Paul calls Jesus the "New Adam," who by his obedient death liberated us from enslavement to sin and offered grace for all (Rom 5:15). For Mark, the death of Jesus was a vicarious sacrifice offered for many (see 14:24). For Luke, the entire life of Jesus, culminating in his death and resurrection, released the transforming power of the Holy Spirit into the world (see 22:49). John presents Jesus as the light who overcomes the darkness of deception and death (see 1:1–18). The Letter to the Hebrews portrays Jesus as the high priest who offers sacrifice to cleanse us from the defilement of sin (4:14-16).

Contemporary theology treats the role of Christ in the work of salvation under the heading of "soteriology." Historically, Anselm of Canterbury (d. 1109) proposed a satisfaction theory that reflected the norms of his feudal society, which measured the gravity of an offense by the status of the one offended. From this perspective, human sin is an infinite offense because it offends the honor of almighty God. Only a God-man could make satisfaction for this infinite offense. By his death, Jesus, substituting for us, offered satisfaction to God, thereby redeeming all humanity.

In the twentieth century, Karl Rahner criticized popular satisfaction theories for making God sound like an angry tyrant demanding horrible suffering from Jesus. As an alternative, Rahner stressed that the merciful God has always sought the salvation of all human beings. To this end, God sent his only Son into the world for our salvation. By his obedient death and glorious resurrection, Jesus Christ, representing the whole human family, has made definitive and irrevocable the final triumph of God's saving will over all that is sinful. Rahner summarizes his distinctive soteriology: "We are saved because this man who is one of us has been saved by God." The resurrection, therefore, is the guarantee that the seeds of the final victory have indeed been planted and that human history will one day reach its goal of union with God.

*How does belief that Christ died "for our sake" strengthen our hope that we can manage the challenges of our complex world?*

# CHRIST SUFFERED DEATH AND WAS BURIED

The Creed simply states that Christ, who was crucified under Pilate, "suffered death and was buried." This brief factual statement could send us back to the Gospels for reflection on the familiar story that can touch our heart and stir our imagination.

The Synoptic Gospels tell us that darkness covered the whole land from the sixth to the ninth hour (noon to 3:00 p.m.), suggesting that the death of Jesus had cosmic significance. In Luke's Gospel, Jesus, though suffering the intense agony of crucifixion, forgave the repentant criminal with the comforting words: "Truly I tell you, today you will be with me in Paradise" (23:43). Both Mark and Matthew report that at the ninth hour, Jesus cried out in a loud voice, "My God, my God, why have you forsaken me?" (Mark 15:34; Matt 27:46). For Luke the final words of Jesus were, "Father, into your hands I commend my spirit" (Luke 23:46).

In John's Gospel, Jesus, right before he dies, commends his mother Mary to the care of the Beloved Disciple (19:25–27). John also reports that near the end Jesus said, "I am thirsty," and after taking the wine raised to his lips, declared, "Now it is finished." Then he bowed his head and delivered over his spirit (19:28–30). Mark and Matthew report that the centurion, who witnessed the death of Jesus exclaimed, "Truly this man was the Son of God" (Mark 15:39; Matt 27:54). Luke has the centurion praise God and proclaim that Jesus was an "innocent man" (Luke 23:47).

All four Gospels tell us about Joseph of Arimathea, a respected member of the council and a secret follower of Jesus, who, with permission from Pilate, buried Jesus in a tomb hewn out of rock and rolled a large stone over the entrance. Mary Magdalene and one of the other Galilean women who traveled with Jesus saw where he was buried. John adds the detail that Nicodemus, who had secretly sought out Jesus, assisted in a traditional Jewish burial (19:38–42).

From the four evangelists we get a substantially consistent portrayal of the death and burial of Jesus. The similarities in the accounts reflect the same sources; the differences reflect the theology of the individual author. For example, Luke's addition to Mark of the story of the repentant thief accords with his general emphasis on forgiveness throughout his Gospel, as in the parable of the prodigal son.

The Creed states the historical fact that Jesus died and was buried. The Gospel accounts tell a story with an inherent power to stimulate personal reflection and spiritual growth.

*How can reflection on the death and burial of Jesus prepare us to carry the crosses imposed by the world today?*

# ON THE THIRD DAY JESUS ROSE AGAIN

The resurrection is the key component of authentic Christian faith. It transforms the darkness of death into the light of new life. It reveals that the somber celebration of Good Friday is really a preparation for the joyful celebration of Easter. The credal statement follows closely First Corinthians where Paul repeats the tradition that "Christ died for our sins and was buried and rose on the third day." He goes on to say that "if Christ had not been raised, our preaching is void of content and your faith is empty too" (1 Cor 15:3–4, 14). The credibility and power of Christian faith rests on the conviction that God has raised Jesus to life.

One way the Gospels present the resurrection is by stories of Mary Magdala, Peter, and the Beloved Disciple discovering the tomb where Jesus was buried to be empty. The other is by reporting appearances of the risen Christ to various people, including Mary Magdala, the eleven disciples, Thomas the twin, and Cleopas and his companion on the road to Emmaus. The appearances are especially striking because the risen Christ presents himself as a forgiving Lord, who brings peace, enlightenment, and renewed hope to his extremely disappointed disciples.

God raising Jesus to a new glorified life validates the life and message of Jesus and vindicates his claim to be the absolute savior charged with the mission to establish the reign of God in the world. The resurrection assures us of fundamental Christian truths: that God is always faithful to the divine promises, that genuine human love is not foolish but survives death itself, that grace is more powerful than sin, and that the seeds of the ultimate triumph of good over evil have been planted. The dogma of the resurrection enables us to believe what we desperately hope is true: that our lives have permanent validity and that all our efforts to love God and neighbor are never wasted.

The resurrection is like a second Big Bang that released an inexhaustible spiritual energy into the world that sustains and guides not only Christian believers but all human beings. When shared, this spiritual energy is not diminished but multiplies. Ultimately the positive energy released by the risen Christ will prevail over all the negative forces that threaten us on our spiritual journey.

*How does belief in the resurrection enable Christians to overcome the dark forces that continue to threaten us today?*

# IN ACCORDANCE WITH THE SCRIPTURES

After confessing that Christ rose again on the third day, the Creed adds, "in accordance with the Scriptures" (see 1 Cor 15:1–4). The Hebrew scriptures clearly did not foretell or contemplate the resurrection of Christ. Perhaps Paul, given his personal encounter with the risen Christ, was referring to the prophet Isaiah, who, after describing the plight of the Suffering Servant, declares, "Out of his anguish he shall see light" (Isa 53:11). He may also have recalled the psalm that praises God who does "not give me up to Sheol, or let your faithful one see the Pit. You show me the path of life" (Ps 16:10–11).

Regarding the "third day," Matthew reports Jesus as saying, "Just as Jonah was three days and three nights in the belly of the sea monster, so for three days and three nights the Son of Man will be in the heart of the earth" (Matt 12:40). And in the Hebrew scriptures, the prophet Hosea calls his people to repentance, assuring them of God's promise that "on the third day he will raise us up, that we may live before him" (Hos 6:2). Paul, who knew Christ was alive, may have found a fuller sense in this text beyond the intent of the author.

This discussion raises the issue of the general relationship between creeds and scripture. We know the early Christian community composed short creeds for the celebration of baptisms, some even before the earliest books of the New Testament were written around AD 50. We also know that the Nicene Creed— written in the fourth century—draws on the images and quotes from the Christian scriptures. The Creed serves as a guide for reading the scriptures by reminding us of the divine nature of Jesus, the protagonist, and by providing an overview of Christ's role in the story of salvation. According to the Nicene Creed, the Word, dwelling in heavenly bliss with the Father, descended to earth, taking the form of a servant, and then through his death and resurrection ascended back to heaven where he sits at the right hand of the Father.

This story of Christ descending and then ascending provides us with a key for interpreting some ambiguous passages in the New Testament. For example, in Philippians, we read that Christ humbled himself to the point of death on a cross, followed by the statement "therefore God also highly exalted him" (Phil 2:6–11). It would be logical to interpret this text as an indication that Christ was not fully God but was raised to an exalted state after his obedient death. The Creed's overview, however, reminds us that it was the originally glorified and then humbled Christ who was exalted, thus preserving his eternal divinity. As we have seen, the Nicene Creed draws on the normative scriptures *and* helps interpret ambiguous passages.

*How can the Creed help us get more out of the scriptures as inspiration for developing a relevant contemporary spirituality?*

# CHRIST ASCENDED INTO HEAVEN

Luke presents two versions of the ascension of Jesus. At the end of his Gospel, he tells us that Jesus led his disciples out of Jerusalem to Bethany, where he gave them a final blessing and "withdrew from them and was carried up into heaven" (Luke 24:51). In the beginning of his second volume, the Acts of the Apostles, the risen Christ promises the apostles that they will receive the Holy Spirit to be his witnesses to the ends of the earth and then "was lifted up, and a cloud took him out of their sight" (Acts 1:9). Two men dressed in white then appeared and told the disciples looking up at the skies, "This Jesus, who has been taken up from you into heaven, will come in the same way as you saw him go into heaven" (Acts 1:6–11).

In John, who emphasizes the descent of the Word from heaven to earth, Jesus tells his disciples, "I came from the Father and have come into the world; again, I am leaving the world and am going to the Father" (John 16:28). When the risen Christ appeared to Mary Magdalene in the garden, he told her, "I am ascending to my Father and your Father, to my God and your God" (John 20:17).

In referring to Christ, the Letter to the Ephesians declares, "He who descended is the same one who ascended far above all the heavens, so that he might fill all things" (Eph 4:10). The Nicene Creed preserves this pattern of descent followed by ascent that is commonly assumed in the New Testament.

The ascension makes it clear that the resurrection of Christ was not a resuscitation of his dead body. It was a totally different event from Jesus raising Lazarus, who resumed his previous life and remained subject to death. The risen Christ did not resume his former life, nor was he again subject to death.

Taken literally, the Lucan portrayal of the ascension makes it seem like Jesus left us, going up to the heavens. Modern science, however, makes it impossible to accept a literal interpretation of this account and turns our attention to the meaning of the ascension. Far from suggesting absence, it affirms the continuing presence of Christ in and through the Holy Spirit sent to all human beings. We recall that Jesus told his disciples it was better for them that he go away because he would send the Advocate to be with them (see John 16:7). We carry Christ's Spirit with us wherever we go, and that Spirit is an inexhaustible source of enlightenment and spiritual energy. During his years on earth, Jesus was confined to a tiny space for a brief time. Now the ascended Christ is present to all people in all places and times. Karl Rahner called the ascension "the universal event of salvation history," which gives us hope when "the lights of the world grow dark," clearly a much-needed message in today's difficult times.

*How does our belief in the ascension of Christ help us manage the complex ambiguities of contemporary society?*

# SEATED AT THE RIGHT HAND OF THE FATHER

The metaphor of the "right hand" appears in the Psalms: "The Lord says to my lord: 'Sit at my right hand until I make your enemies your footstool'" (Ps 110:1); and "The right hand of the Lord is exalted; the right hand of the Lord does valiantly" (Ps 118:16).

The New Testament makes use of this imagery in several places. For example, writing late in the first century, the First Letter of Peter explains that baptism connects us to the risen Christ "who has gone into heaven and is at the right hand of God, with angels, authorities, and powers made subject to him" (1 Pet 3:21–22). Luke's Gospel tells us that Jesus in his trial before the Sanhedrin tells his accusers, "From now on the Son of Man will be seated at the right hand of the power of God" (Luke 22:69).

At the right hand of God, the risen Christ shares in the divine power over the whole created world. All things are subject to his authority, including the devil and the enemies of the good God. During his time on earth, Jesus performed many exorcisms of the demons he encountered in his ministry, demonstrating his power over Satan. Now, as the risen Lord at God's right hand, Christ has power over all the demonic forces anywhere on earth. This power is already at work in our world today but will be completed only at the end time when all his enemies are under his feet.

Christ's ascent to God's right hand is the fulfillment of the prophecy in the Book of Daniel where it states that the dominion of the Son of Man over all people is an "everlasting dominion that shall not pass away, and his kingship is one that shall never be destroyed" (Dan 7:14). Faith in the everlasting dominion of Christ alerts us to the small victories of good over evil in our daily lives.

Christ's presence at God's right hand not only gives us confidence in the fight against evil but also reminds us that our ascended Lord continues to intercede with God on our behalf. We have a friend in the highest places. Christ—with his personal experience of the human condition—is on our side as we strive to become our best self, to activate our potential, and to grow spiritually. When we make progress, prayers of gratitude to our brother with God are in order; when we are discouraged, we can turn to our mediator for help and hope. Eyes of faith detect the enthroned Christ in our graced moments of life: a loved one makes us feel special; a friend is there when needed; a colleague offers helpful advice; a stranger surprises us with kindness.

*How can Christ's presence at God's right hand help us improve our personal relations?*

# CHRIST WILL COME AGAIN

Among the early Christians, there was a general expectation that the risen Lord would return soon. The earliest New Testament text, Paul's First Letter to the Thessalonians (ca. AD 50), mentions a return of the Lord Jesus to deliver us from "the wrath that is coming" (1:10). The Gospel of Mark declares that "this generation will not pass away until all these things have taken place" (Mark 13:30). Matthew repeats the main ideas of Mark but adds that Jesus will come again as the judge of the living and the dead (see Matt 25:1–46). Describing the end time, Matthew says, "When the Son of Man comes in his glory, and all the angels with him, then he will sit on the throne of his glory" (v. 31). As the judge, Christ will welcome into the kingdom those who have attended to the hungry and thirsty and will dismiss those who did not (vv. 32–45).

As time went on, especially after the destruction of Jerusalem in AD 70, Christians had to deal with the "delayed Parousia," the Greek word used in the New Testament for the second coming of Christ. The Second Letter of Peter, probably written in the first decade of the second century, deals explicitly with this issue. Convinced that Christ will return, the author explains that the delay is for the good, allowing time for all people to repent. Besides, the author tells us, "With the Lord one day is like a thousand years, and a thousand years are like one day" (2 Pet 3:8). We must be alert because "the Lord will come like a thief" to establish "new heavens and a new earth, where righteousness is at home" (2 Pet 3:10–13).

As we seek to understand the dogma of the Parousia, it is important to distinguish the core belief expressed in the Creed from the imagery used in the New Testament. Our fundamental belief is that Christ will complete his saving work, as promised, at some essentially unknowable future time. Those Christians who have used biblical imagery to predict the exact day of the Parousia have neglected the fact that Jesus himself said he did not know the day or hour when the end time would come. Furthermore, thinking of the Parousia as a return can be misleading, since it sounds like Christ left us, which is not the case. It is more accurate to speak about Christ ultimately completing his saving work. While some Christians today eagerly await the Lord's return, most of us are not emotionally engaged in this belief. The teaching becomes more meaningful when it alerts us to ways that the risen Christ is spreading the kingdom of love and peace in our world today, as preparation for the final victory of good over evil in the Parousia.

*How can belief in the Parousia encourage us to seize the opportunities for spiritual growth today?*

# CHRIST'S KINGDOM WILL HAVE NO END

The Bible is filled with kingdom imagery. The Hebrew scriptures speak of Yahweh as "a great King above all gods" (Ps 95:3), whose name "is great among the nations" (Mal 1:11). In the beginning of Luke's Gospel, the angel Gabriel tells Mary that her son Jesus "will reign over the house of Jacob forever, and of his kingdom there will be no end" (Luke 1:31–33). The Synoptic Gospels use the metaphor of the "kingdom of God," or its equivalents "kingdom of heaven" and "reign of God," some eighty times in describing the message and mission of Jesus. Many passages suggest the kingdom is already present, as indicated by these statements of Jesus: "The kingdom of heaven has come near" (Matt 3:2); "the kingdom of God is among you" (Luke 17:21); and "If it is by the Spirit of God that I cast out demons, then the kingdom of God has come to you" (Matt 12:28).

The kingdom was already present in Jesus himself and in his ministry. He understood himself as the absolute savior, uniquely called to establish and extend the reign of God in the world. His cures and exorcisms were visible signs that God's healing power was available for persons in need. His reaching out to the lepers and welcoming women to his ministry were signs of the inclusive nature of God's reign. The forgiveness Jesus offered to repentant sinners served as a constant reminder that divine mercy is available in the world.

In these ways, the word "reign" functioned as a metaphor illuminating God's mysterious, intimate relationship with human beings. It is not a geographical territory or an intellectual concept but a symbol that gives rise to further thoughtful reflection. The reign of God cannot be identified with any political entity, though it can inspire efforts to create a more just political order. Nor can it be identified with the Church, though the faith community is called to be a sign and instrument of God's reign in the world.

The New Testament views the reign of God not only as a present reality operative in our world but also as a future reality that will be complete only at the end time. For example, Jesus taught us to pray "thy kingdom come," suggesting it is a future reality. The parable about waiting until harvest time to separate the weeds and the wheat suggests that the final triumph of good over evil is a future event (see Matt 13:24–30). For Mark, the total triumph of God's reign will be a future event, unknown even to himself but only to the Father (see Mark 13:32).

Christian faith holds in tension two convictions: the reign of God is already here operating in our lives, and it will be completed only at an unknown end time. Faced with the enduring evil in our world, this twofold belief grounds our hope that the good will ultimately prevail over evil and alerts us to God's mercy and love in our troubled world today.

*How can the biblical teaching on the "reign of God" maintain our work for greater justice and peace in today's world?*

# THE HOLY SPIRIT

The third main section of the Nicene Creed regarding belief in the Holy Spirit was not in the original version produced by the Council of Nicaea in 325. It was promulgated in 381 by the First Council of Constantinople, called by Emperor Theodosius to help unify his empire badly divided by the Arian heresy. Some 186 Eastern bishops (none from the West) participated in the council, and all but thirty-six committed to Nicene orthodoxy. In drafting what came to be called the "Nicene-Constantinopolitan Creed," the bishops drew on existing baptismal creeds that included statements defending the divinity of the Holy Spirit against some radical Arians.

The Bible depicts the Spirit in many ways that defy easy classification. In the Hebrew scriptures, the Psalmist prays to God, "Do not take your holy spirit from me" (51:11), and the prophet Joel has God declare, "I will pour out my spirit on all flesh; your sons and your daughters shall prophesy, your old men shall dream dreams, and your young men shall see visions" (Joel 2:28).

In the New Testament, Paul presents the Holy Spirit as a power that dwells in us (see Rom 15:13), making us children of God and coheirs with Christ (see Rom 8:14–17). The Holy Spirit plays an important role in the Gospels: overshadowing Mary's conception of Jesus (see Luke 1:55), assuring Simeon that he would see the Messiah (see Luke 2:20), descending on Jesus at his baptism by John (see Mark 1:12–13), leading Jesus to return to Galilee after his temptation (Luke 4:14), anointing Jesus to preach the good news to the poor (Luke 4:18), reminding disciples what

Jesus taught them (see John 14:26), and speaking for the disciples when they are brought to trial (see Matt 10:20). In the Acts of the Apostles, the Holy Spirit guides the development of the early Church: descending on the apostles at Pentecost (see 2:1–4), moving the Jewish Christians to accept Gentiles (see 10:38–47), and directing Paul's ministry (see 16:6–7).

The New Testament also has references to the Holy Spirit that suggest unity and equality with the Father and the Son. At the end of his Second Letter to the Corinthians, Paul writes a farewell: "The grace of the Lord Jesus Christ, the love of God, and the communion of the Holy Spirit be with all of you" (2 Cor 13:13). In Matthew, the risen Christ commissions his disciples: "All authority in heaven and on earth has been given to me. Go therefore and make disciples of all nations, baptizing them in the name of the Father and of the Son and of the Holy Spirit, and teaching them to obey everything that I have commanded you. And remember, I am with you always, to the end of the age" (Matt 28:18–20).

The Nicene Creed promulgated by the Council of Constantinople in 381 was formulated to affirm the true divinity of the Holy Spirit. It invites us to give the Holy Spirit a more prominent role in our spirituality. Pope John Paul II encouraged us in the West to breathe out of both lungs by appropriating more of the spirituality of Eastern Christians, who have preserved a deeper appreciation of the power of the Holy Spirit in their piety. This advice of the pope seems more important today than ever.

*How can we be more open to the Holy Spirit in developing a viable contemporary spirituality?*

# THE LORD, THE GIVER OF LIFE

The Arian heresy, which denied the full divinity of the Word made flesh, claimed that the Holy Spirit was created by

God through the Son and was, therefore, a creature and not fully God. This heresy, sometimes called Macedonianism, was not addressed at the Council of Nicaea in 325 and became more widespread during the fourth century, contributing to the disruption of the Roman Empire.

At the First Council of Constantinople in 381, Nicene theologians looked for ways to affirm the full divinity of the Holy Spirit. Gregory Nazianzus (329–389), one of the three Cappadocian fathers, along with Basil the Great and his younger brother Gregory of Nyssa, proposed using the same approach adapted by Nicaea to defend the divinity of Christ by declaring that the Holy Spirit is one substance (*homoousios*) with the Father. We do not have a record of the debates at the council, but we know from the final text that the bishops decided to use more biblical language to define the divinity of the Holy Spirit.

The council's decisive move was to name the Holy Spirit "Lord," the English translation of the Greek word *kyrios*, used for God in the Greek version of the Old Testament. In the New Testament, Christ is called "Lord" numerous times, sometimes indicating his divinity. For example, in his Letter to the Philippians, Paul says that "every tongue should confess that Jesus Christ is Lord, to the glory of God the Father" (Phil 2:11). In this context, the creedal statement naming the Holy Spirit "Lord" is an affirmation of divinity, making the Holy Spirit equal to the Father and the Son. In this way, the Creed grounds a trinitarian monotheism, belief in one God with three persons: Father, Son, and Holy Spirit.

The Creed goes on to affirm the Holy Spirit is "the giver of life." The Hebrew scriptures portray God as the source of life. For example, in Deuteronomy, God says, "I kill and I make alive" (Deut 32:39), and the Psalmist praises God, proclaiming, "For with you is the fountain of life" (Ps 36:9). In the New Testament,

Jesus declares, "I came that they may have life, and have it abundantly" (John 10:10), suggesting Christ's divine power.

The New Testament also sees the Holy Spirit as a giver of life. The Spirit overshadowed Mary and she conceived new life (see Luke 1:26–38). Later, the Spirit descended on Jesus at his baptism, propelling him into his public life (see Mark 1:9–13). In Galatians, Paul declares, "If you sow to the Spirit, you will reap eternal life from the Spirit" (Gal 6:8). At Pentecost, the Holy Spirit descended on the disciples, who boldly proclaimed the good news of the risen Christ as the Spirit prompted them. Then Peter stood and gave a sermon, explaining that the risen Lord, who first received the promised Holy Spirit from the Father, has "poured this Spirit out on us" (Acts 2:1–41). The Creed invites us to reflect on the Holy Spirit as the Source of life and, therefore, truly God.

*How can reflection on the Holy Spirit as Lord, the giver of life, help us to be more faithful and responsible Christian in today's increasingly secular culture?*

# THE SPIRIT PROCEEDS FROM THE FATHER AND THE SON

After affirming that the Holy Spirit is the Lord, the giver of life, the Creed adds "who proceeds from the Father and the Son," which centuries later became its most controversial statement. In 381, the 186 bishops from the eastern part of the Roman Empire debated the section on the Holy Spirit without input or approval from Pope Damasus I or any western bishops. Drawing on existing baptismal formulas used in eastern churches, the council adopted the statement "who proceeds from the Father."

The scriptural basis for this creedal statement is found in the farewell discourse of Jesus at the Last Supper, where he talks about the Paraclete, "the Spirit of truth who comes from the Father" (John 15:26). Other passages support this position. For example, in Luke, Jesus assures his disciples that their heavenly Father will give the Holy Spirit to those who ask (see Luke 11:13). By declaring that the Holy Spirit is "the Lord, the giver of life," the Creed affirms the procession of the Spirit from the Father without undercutting the true divinity of the Holy Spirit.

The controversy over this article of the Creed became public when in 589, at the Third Council of Toledo in Spain, the Latin phrase *filioque* (and the Son) was added to the official Creed. This addition reflected the view of western theologians, including Augustine (d. 430), who taught that the Holy Spirit proceeds from the Father and the Son, although "principally" from the Father. There is scriptural justification for this position. In John's Gospel, for instance, Jesus tells his disciples, "I tell you the truth: it is to your advantage that I go away, for if I do not go away, the Advocate will not come to you" (John 16:7). During the reign of Emperor Charlemagne (800–814), Masses at the court included *filioque* in the Creed, and in 1014, Pope Benedict VIII included it in the Creed recited at Rome.

In the East, the Patriarch of Constantinople, Photius (d. ca. 893), influenced by political considerations, declared the *filioque* addition to be illegitimate and theologically erroneous. In the following centuries the *filioque* controversy intensified and was a contributing factor to the decisive split between the Eastern Orthodox and Roman Catholic Churches in 1054, which has remained to this day, although the mutual excommunications were lifted in 1965 by Pope Paul VI and Patriarch Athenagoras of Constantinople.

Today, very few Western Christians understand this controversy or care about it. There are, however, important lessons to be learned from it. Political considerations can easily distort the quest for religious truth. There is no unsolvable theological reason for maintaining the institutional divide between the Orthodox and Catholic churches. The Orthodox churches have validly ordained priests and bishops and validly celebrate all seven sacraments. Theology should illumine fundamental Christian truths, not obscure them. The unification of Eastern and Western churches would enhance the Christian witness to our badly divided world. Let us pray that Church leaders will find a way to bring about this much needed and long-awaited reconciliation.

*How can greater Christian unity help overcome the divisive polarization that continues to plague our country and world?*

# WORSHIPED AND GLORIFIED

The Bible insists that only God is to be worshiped and glorified. When tempted by Satan to worship the devil, Jesus quoted Deuteronomy 6:13: "Worship the Lord your God, and serve only him" (Matt 4:10). This verse is typical of the Hebrew scriptures, which connect genuine worship with service. The New Testament speaks of worshiping God. For example, Paul says a repentant unbeliever will fall prostrate and worship God, crying out, "God is really among you" (1 Cor 14:25), and the Book of Revelation says explicitly, "Worship God!" (Rev 22:9).

The Gospels also indicate that the risen Christ is worthy of worship. Matthew, for example, tells us that Mary Magdalene and "the other Mary" embraced the feet of the risen Lord and "worshiped him" (Matt 28:9). Nowhere, however, does the New Testament speak about worshiping the Holy Spirit. Therefore, the creedal statement about worshiping the Spirit represents a development of doctrine during the early centuries of the Christian era, affirming the full divinity of the Holy Spirit.

The word "glory" appears frequently in the Bible, in many cases representing an attribute of God who is majestic and powerful.

For example, the "glory of the Lord" settled upon Mount Sinai as God prepared to give Moses the Ten Commandments (see Exod 24:16). In the New Testament, God's glory was manifested in the transfiguration of Jesus (see Mark 9:2–8). In John's Gospel, Jesus speaks of revealing the Father's glory (see John 17:1–5).

The other use of "glory" refers to our obligation to acknowledge God's glory. King Herod died when he failed to give glory to God (see Acts 12:23). The First Letter of Timothy includes this liturgical prayer: "To the King of the ages, immortal, invisible, the only God, be honor and glory forever and ever" (1 Tim 1:17). Paul's letter to the Galatians includes a greeting from God our Father "to whom be the glory forever and ever" (Gal 1:3–5). In a vision of heavenly worship, the Book of Revelation says twenty-four elders sing, "You are worthy, our Lord and God, to receive glory and honor and power" (Rev 4:11). Again, the New Testament says nothing about glorification of the Holy Spirit, but the fourth-century Creed reflects the developed faith of the Christian community that the Holy Spirit is divine and worthy of glory.

We have various ways of giving glory to the Holy Spirit. Liturgically, we pray to the Father through the Son in union with the Holy Spirit. In our private prayer, we follow the promptings of the Spirit. We honor the Holy Spirit by following the Spirit's guidance in our daily lives. We offer praise to the Advocate by actively working for peace and justice. The Spirit is glorified through honest dialogue in the pursuit of truth. We acknowledge the power of the Paraclete by sanctifying everyday life and using our gifts to serve the common good. Glorifying the Holy Spirit unites all Christians in the common effort to transform the darkness of tragedy into the light of renewed life.

*How can we expand our efforts to worship and glorify the Holy Spirit in our secularized culture?*

# THE HOLY SPIRIT HAS SPOKEN THROUGH THE PROPHETS

*The Catechism of the Catholic Church* understands "prophets" to include "all whom the Holy Spirit inspired in the composition of the sacred books, both of the Old and New Testament" (§702).

The Holy Spirit spoke through Israel's great leaders (Abraham, Moses, and David) as well as through her major prophets (Isaiah, Jeremiah, and Ezekiel). In the New Testament, the Spirit spoke through the prophets Simeon and Anna, who identified the infant Jesus as the Messiah, and through John the Baptist, who recognized Jesus as the true leader of Israel's reform. We can think of Mary of Magdala as a prophetic witness to the risen Christ, who sent her to tell his other disciples the good news. At Pentecost, the Holy Spirit descended on the apostles and inspired Peter to preach a powerful sermon that led to the baptism of three thousand Christian converts that day. The Holy Spirit also spoke through Paul of Tarsus, who found creative ways of spreading the good news of a Jewish Messiah—crucified and risen—to the Gentile world, where it flourished.

The Holy Spirit, who spoke through the scriptures, has continued throughout history to speak through inspired prophets, including Athanasius of Alexandria (d. 363), the great champion of Nicene orthodoxy during the turbulent fourth century. In 325, as a twenty-seven-year-old deacon at the Council of Nicaea, he helped get the bishops to declare Christ as *homoousios*, that is, "one in substance" with the Father, that defined orthodoxy against the Arian heresy. Three years after the council, after strong public acclamation, he was elected archbishop and patriarch of Alexandria, a position he held intermittently for the remaining forty-eight years of his life. Although he was constantly under attack and sent into exile on five separate occasions (more than seventeen years in total) by Arian-leaning emperors and bishops, he remained faithful to the Nicene Creed. He wrote many books, including ascetical works, such as the *Life of St. Antony*, and theological treatises, for example, *On the Incarnation*, defending the full divinity of Christ and the Holy Spirit. In 1508, he was proclaimed one of the great Doctors of the Eastern Church, and his feast is now celebrated on May 2.

Gregory of Nazianzus, himself a Doctor of the Church, called Athanasius "the true pillar of the Church" and said, "His life and conduct were the rule of bishops, and his doctrine the rule of orthodox faith." The recently canonized Cardinal John Henry Newman lauded Athanasius as "a principal instrument, after the Apostles, by which the sacred truths of Christianity have been conveyed and secured to the world." The Holy Spirit has indeed spoken through great people like Isaiah, Paul, Athanasius, and many more celebrated and unsung prophets throughout history.

*Which prophets are most helpful to me in the ongoing struggle against lingering prejudices?*

# THE CHURCH IS ONE

The Council of Constantinople identified the Church founded by Christ as "one, holy, catholic, and apostolic." These four properties of the Church are gifts given by God through Christ in union with the Holy Spirit to form the People of God, the Body of Christ, and the Temple of the Spirit. They also function as ideals to guide the development of the Church as it strives to be a credible sign and effective instrument of God's reign. The Church as we experience it always falls short of those ideal properties, which motivates us to participate in the ongoing purification of the

Church. The graced but sinful Church must always be renewing itself. The four properties of the Church set a direction and goal for practical efforts to make the Church a more effective witness to Christ's continuing presence in the world.

The claim and hope that the Church is "one" recalls Jesus saying to God the Father, "There will be one flock, one shepherd" (John 10:16). Later in John's Gospel, Jesus prays, "I ask not only on behalf of these, but also on behalf of those who will believe in me through their word, that they may all be one. As you, Father, are in me and I am in you" (John 17:20–21). In the Acts of the Apostles, Luke presents an idealized picture of the original Christian community, where believers shared "all things in common," "spent much time together in the temple," and "broke bread at home and ate their food with glad and generous hearts" (see Acts 2:42–47). The Letter to the Ephesians identifies the fundamental unity of all Christians, saying, "There is one body and one Spirit...one Lord, one faith, one baptism, one God the Father of all," and encourages them to make "every effort to maintain the unity of the Spirit in the bond of peace" (Eph 4:3–6).

Unfortunately, as Christians, we have failed throughout history to maintain the gift of unity, contributing to various disputes, heresies, and schisms. As noted earlier, a major split occurred in 1054 when the Eastern Orthodox Church and the Western Roman Catholic Church mutually excommunicated each other. The other major division happened in the sixteenth century with the break between the Catholic Church and various Protestant churches, which continues to this day.

The modern ecumenical movement, which gained momentum in the twentieth century and was spurred by the Second Vatican Council, has sought to overcome divisions and to restore the unity envisioned by Christ. Definite progress has been achieved with the mutual lifting of the 1054 excommunications and substantive agreement between the Catholic Church and mainline Protestant churches on the major issue of justification, which divided them for centuries. Progress was made when the churches put less emphasis on the four marks as proof of their claim to be the true church of Christ and, instead, used them as ideal properties that call for reform and renewal of all churches, bringing them closer to Christ and to one another. Reciting the Creed together at worship reminds us of our responsibility to help further the ecumenical movement and move the Church closer to being truly "one."

*How can I promote ecumenical dialogue and collaboration in our fragmented world?*

# THE CHURCH IS HOLY

The word "holy" points to a property of the Church as well as an ideal to be sought. In the Book of Leviticus, God declares, "For I am the LORD your God; sanctify yourselves therefore, and be holy, for I am holy" (Lev 11:44). This call to holiness directed to all the People of God is continued in the New Testament. In his First Letter to the Thessalonians, Paul declares, "This is the will of God, your sanctification: that you abstain from fornication" (1 Thess 4:3). For Paul, the call to holiness is addressed not to a privileged group in the Church but to "all God's beloved" (Rom 1:7).

The Letter to the Ephesians makes it clear that Christ gave himself up for the whole Church "to make her holy by cleansing her with the washing of water by the word, so as to present the church to himself in splendor, without a spot or wrinkle or anything of the kind" (Eph 5:25–27). Paul's letters also indicate that Christ's gift of holiness was often thwarted by human sinfulness. For example, First Corinthians speaks of "quarrels" that introduced "divisions" in the Church (1 Cor 1:10–17).

Blessed by Christ's gift of the Spirit, the Church has a vast reservoir of spiritual resources: the scriptures that instruct and inspire us; the sacraments that provide encounters with Christ at crucial moments in our life; the doctrines and creeds that guide orthodox belief; the saints, who inspire commitment to Christ; and the growing body of social teaching that promotes the cause of justice and peace.

Some of the Church's resources are especially relevant for humanizing contemporary culture: a communal sense of human existence that challenges rugged individualism; ascetical practices that challenge consumerism and hedonism; and an appreciation of the mystery in human affairs that challenges one-dimensional secularism.

Today, talk of a holy Church contrasts with the reality of the horrendous sex-abuse scandal. Not only have priests, called to be servant leaders of the community, abused minors, some repeatedly, but some bishops charged with an oversight role have covered up cases of abuse to preserve the appearance of holiness in the institutional Church. The scandal has sadly risen to the highest levels of the Church. Pope John Paul II, for example, failed to do anything about the long-standing, well-documented abusive behavior of Marcial Maciel, the founder of the Legion of Christ and the Regnum Christi movement; and Pope Francis admitted to initially mishandling the abuse scandal in Chile by failing to listen to the cries of victims.

There is no easy defense of the holiness of the Church or glib words that restore confidence in the institution. We can hope and pray that the Spirit, who guides the Church, will prove more powerful than the sin that distorts its witness, that the Church's valuable spiritual resources will penetrate the darkness of scandal and help sanctify individuals and the community, and that the decentralized synodal approach of Pope Francis will be effective in managing the crisis and revealing the hidden holiness of the

Church. Not many of us can say we have done all we could to protect and assist victims and challenge complicit bishops.

*What can we do to make the Church a more credible witness to holiness in our skeptical world?*

# THE CHURCH IS CATHOLIC

According to the *Catechism of the Catholic Church*, "catholic" means "universal" in the sense of "in keeping with the whole." The Church is catholic because it is the Body of Christ, commissioned by God to bring salvation to the whole human family. The risen Christ mandated his followers, "Go therefore and make disciples of all nations, baptizing them in the name of the Father and of the Son and of the Holy Spirit, and teaching them to obey everything that I have commanded you. And remember, I am with you always, to the end of the age" (Matt 28:19–20).

Since God "desires everyone to be saved" (1 Tim 2:4), the Church has a universal mission to establish a "particular church" in all lands and cultures. Jesus Christ, the definitive prophet, has universal significance, and his Gospel can be planted and flourish in diverse cultures. Today, after two thousand years of evangelization, Christians make up about 31 percent of the world's population, with most of the current growth occurring in the "global south," Africa, Asia, and Latin America. In terms of extension, catholicity remains an ideal only partially achieved and awaiting fulfillment at the end time.

Catholicity also refers to inclusivity, the fundamental openness of the Church to diversity. By example and word, Jesus modeled inclusive catholicity. He included in his ministry Galilean fisherman, despised tax collectors, and political zealots. Despite breaking social taboos, he publicly engaged women in religious conversation and reached out to lepers banished to the margins.

His parable of the good Samaritan made a despised enemy the hero of the story. While generally confining his mission to the Jewish community, he did accede to the clever requests of a Gentile woman and cured her daughter. His table fellowship with sinners scandalized some but reflected the confidence Jesus had that the mercy of God was intended for all people. During his passion, Jesus reinforced this teaching by forgiving his executioners and the repentant thief.

About two decades after the death of Jesus, the leaders of his movement made the crucial decision to allow Gentile converts to join the community without imposing on them the observance of Jewish law. Saint Paul expressed the fundamental warrant for inclusive catholicity in his letter to the Galatians: "There is no longer Jew or Greek, there is no longer slave or free, there is no longer male and female; for all of you are one in Christ Jesus" (Gal 3:28). The Letter to the Ephesians expanded the point by assuring Gentile converts that they "are no longer strangers and aliens" but "citizens with the saints and also members of the household of God," forming a building with the apostles and prophets as the foundation and "with Christ Jesus himself as the cornerstone" (Eph 2:19–22). The early decision to open the Church to Gentiles actualized the inclusive teaching of Jesus and serves as a model for the Church today, as it strives to heal a fractured world. The more truly catholic the Church is, the more credible its challenge to all forms of discrimination and tribalism that pit "us" against "them."

*How can I make my parish more inclusively catholic in our sharply divided society?*

# THE CHURCH IS APOSTOLIC

According to the *Catechism*, "apostolic" means that the Church is founded on the apostles and hands on the deposit of faith received from them. Furthermore, the Church continues to be guided by the teaching of the apostles through their successors, the college of bishops, in union with the Bishop of Rome. Mark tells us that Jesus "appointed twelve, whom he also named apostles, to be with him, and to be sent out to proclaim the message" (Mark 3:14). Christ, the emissary of the Father, appointed the apostles as ambassadors to carry on his mission. In the Gospel of John, Jesus says, "As the Father has sent me, so I send you" (John 20:21). From Christ, the apostles received both the mandate to be stewards of God's mysteries and the power to carry out this mission.

The original apostles were the official witnesses of the resurrection of Christ, and their successors, the bishops of the Church, continue to be witness to that original transforming experience. The Second Vatican Council teaches that "the bishops have by divine institution taken the place of the apostles as pastors of the Church" so that "whoever listens to them is listening to Christ" (*Lumen Gentium* 20).

It is important to understand the apostolic ministry of the hierarchy in the larger context of the apostolic role of the whole Church. All the baptized are called to participate in the mission of Christ to spread the reign of God in the world. Scripture, which is our normative access to the apostolic tradition, is a gift given for the benefit of all the faithful, suitable for instruction and encouragement for everyone. Vatican II teaches that the "whole body of the faithful who have an anointing that comes from the holy one cannot err in matters of belief" (*Lumen Gentium* 12).

Historically, we know from the studies of Cardinal Newman and other scholars that, in the fourth century, the Catholic laity remained more faithful to the Nicene orthodox teaching on Christ than many Arian bishops. There is an instinct of faith (*sensus fidei*) that guides members of the Church, through the Holy Spirit, to a proper understanding and appreciation of the apostolic tradition. All members of the Church are called by virtue of their baptism, and not simply by hierarchal delegation, to participate in the apostolate of the Church, making use of their unique gifts.

Apostolicity is both a gift and a call to action. We are privileged to have the Gospels, which give us a substantially correct picture of Jesus and his major teachings, as well as the Epistles, which offer practical advice on how to live as authentic disciples of Christ. We find inspiration in the apostles, Mary of Magdala, and Paul of Tarsus.

The challenge is to make apostolicity more credible by living the Gospel, practicing charity, spreading the reign of God, and working for justice and peace. The earthly Church will always fall short of its highest ideals, but the regular recitation of the Creed keeps before us the four marks of the Church, including "apostolic."

*How can I make the Church more apostolic in a culture weakened by relativism?*

# ONE BAPTISM

After noting the four properties of the Church, the Creed declares, "We acknowledge one baptism." We note the change of verb from "we *believe*," used throughout the whole Creed, to "we *acknowledge*," which some scholars claim denotes an accepted fact of church life not in dispute, as were the previous articles of the Creed calling for belief.

At the time of Jesus, we know that the Essene community of Qumran performed baptismal rituals and that John the Baptist preached and practiced baptism as a sign of repentance for sins. By participating in John's ritual baptism, Jesus signified his readiness to begin his own mission to spread the reign of God. During the public ministry of Jesus, his disciples drew the attention of the Pharisees in Judea by baptizing more disciples than the Baptist (see John 4:2). After his resurrection, Christ commissioned his disciples to make disciples of all nations, "baptizing them in the name of the Father and of the Son and of the Holy Spirit" (Matt 28:19).

Saint Paul helps us understand the deeper meaning of baptism: "For in the one Spirit we were all baptized into one body — Jews or Greeks, slaves or free" (1 Cor 12:13); "All of us who have been baptized into Christ Jesus were baptized into his death" so that "just as Christ was raised from the dead by the glory of the Father, so we too might walk in newness of life" (Rom 6:3–4). In the Church, there is one body, one Spirit, one hope, one Lord, and "one baptism," the phrase used by the Nicene Creed (see Eph 4:4–5).

The Second Vatican Council generated a very fruitful reappropriation of the meaning and purpose of baptism. Through our baptismal incorporation into the Body of Christ, we become full members of the Church, able to share in its rich spiritual resources. By dying and rising with Christ, we drink of his Spirit, who guides and energizes our efforts to follow his commands. By virtue of our baptism, we are all called to follow our unique path to holiness. Our common baptismal vocation is to build up the Body of Christ and extend the reign of God in our sphere of influence. Through baptism, we receive the gifts of the Holy Spirit that we are to use for the common good. As baptized Christians, we share in the priesthood of Christ, empowered to follow his example of self-sacrificing love and to participate in the eucharistic liturgy, offering our gift to the Father through Christ in union with the Holy Spirit.

This theology of baptism makes it clear that there are no second-class citizens in the Church. The priesthood of the baptized has its own inherent gifts and responsibilities, derived not from hierarchical delegation, but from union with Christ himself. As Pope Francis frequently reminds us, top-down solutions to contemporary problems are less likely to be effective in the long run than movements that originate at the grassroots and draw on the wisdom and energy of the faithful living their baptismal priesthood.

*How can fidelity to my baptismal vows help me develop a balanced contemporary spirituality?*

# THE FORGIVENESS OF SINS

Baptism makes visible the ever-available mercy of God and places on us the responsibility to share that gift by forgiving offenders. Jesus Christ, who understood the importance of forgiveness in human affairs better than any other prophet or spiritual guide, provides the most compelling witness to the practice of forgiveness by his example and teaching. In the parable of the prodigal son, Jesus taught us that God's merciful forgiveness is even greater than the father who welcomes back his wayward son not with a reprimand but with a lavish party. His other parables of mercy—the lost sheep and the lost coin—also remind us that God rejoices over the return of the repentant sinner. The prayer Jesus taught us makes an essential connection between receiving forgiveness and extending it: "Forgive us our trespasses as we forgive those who trespass against us." This call to forgiveness extends even to enemies and those who do us harm, as Jesus proclaimed in his great Sermon on the Mount.

The teaching of Jesus on forgiveness gains credibility by his own example. He submitted to John's baptism for the forgiveness of sins, even though he knew himself sinless. He forgave the woman taken in adultery after exposing the sinful hypocrisy of her accusers. During his passion, he forgave his executioners and assured the repentant thief of his place in paradise. After his resurrection, the Lord greeted the apostles who deserted him, not with condemnations, but with reconciling words of peace.

For the original disciples, blessed with Christ's forgiveness, baptism was the ritual expression of this gift. In his powerful sermon on the first Pentecost, Peter admonished the crowd: "Repent, and be baptized every one of you in the name of Jesus Christ so that your sins may be forgiven; and you will receive the gift of the Holy Spirit" (Acts 2:38). When Paul, who was persecuting Christians as Jewish heretics, encountered the risen Lord, he was told, "Get up, be baptized, and have your sins washed away, calling on his name" (Acts 22:16). Forgiveness symbolized in baptism is central to the Christian message.

Our polarized society, which tends to multiple enemies and victims, needs forgiveness and reconciliation. Hardness of heart is dangerous to our health. Resentment can poison our system, and forgiveness is the only effective antidote. Those who think of themselves as perpetual victims of the misdeeds of others can find liberation by forgiving the perpetrators and getting on with their own lives with greater freedom and energy.

Forgiving is not the same as forgetting, nor does it mean condoning sinful behavior. It does mean refusing to identify offenders with their bad behavior and giving them a chance to begin again and construct a better life. Those who offend us are children of God, saved by Christ and animated by the Holy Spirit. Their lives, like our own, are a mix of grace and sin. We might do better at forgiving by pondering the question of Jesus: "Why do you see the speck in your neighbor's eye, but do not notice the log in your own eye?" (Luke 6:41).

*Is there a particular individual I should forgive to fulfill my baptismal responsibility?*

# THE RESURRECTION OF THE DEAD

After stating "I *believe*" in the Church and "I *acknowledge*" one baptism, the Creed uses a third verb, "We *look for* the resurrection of the dead." The Greek original means "expect" and suggests an active sense of anticipation. The earliest reference to the resurrection in the Hebrew scriptures is in Second Maccabees, written around 125 BC, that tells the story of seven Jewish men tortured and killed for refusing to eat pork in violation of the law. Forced to watch this heartbreaking cruelty, their mother assured them that the Creator of the universe "will in his mercy give life and breath back to you again, since you now forget yourselves for the sake of his laws" (2 Macc 7:22–25). By the time of Jesus, the Jewish community was split on belief in the resurrection, with the Sadducees denying it on the grounds that it was not in the original teaching of the scriptures and the Pharisees affirming it as a legitimate development within the Jewish faith. Jesus chided the Sadducees for failing to understand the scriptures, emphasizing that the God of Abraham, Isaiah, and Jacob "is God not of the dead, but of the living" (Mark 12:18–27). In John's Gospel, Jesus solemnly assured his disciples that "the hour is coming, and is now here, when the dead will hear the voice of the Son of God, and those who hear will live" (John 5:25).

Saint Paul offers hope to those grieving the loss of loved ones: "For since we believe that Jesus died and rose again, even so, through Jesus, God will bring with him those who have died" (1 Thess 4:13–18).

Belief in the resurrection is the linchpin of Christian faith. To the Corinthians, Paul argues that if there is no resurrection of the dead "then our proclamation has been in vain and your faith has been in vain." He adds that "if for this life only we have hoped in Christ, we are of all people most to be pitied" (1 Cor 15:13–19).

More positively, belief in the resurrection of the dead means that our earthly journey has a final destination and that our life story is not a tale told by an idiot but a narrative guided by a benign power. The resurrection is the guarantee that all our good efforts in life have a permanent validity, that death is not the end of our conscious life but the passageway to a richer and fuller life, and that we are destined to join our deceased loved ones in the great communion of saints.

Looking forward to the resurrection can boost our spirits in depressing times and help us carry heavy crosses. It can give deeper meaning to ordinary activities and alert us to the dimension of mystery in our daily life. It can move us to concrete deeds of charity to assist those in need who are destined to share in the resurrection of the dead.

*How can belief in the resurrection of the dead help us create a more humane and just society?*

# THE LIFE OF THE WORLD TO COME

The final affirmation of the Nicene Creed looks forward to "the life of the world to come." The New Testament refers to this reality as "eternal life." In one of the best-known verses, John declares, "For God so loved the world that he gave his only Son, so that everyone who believes in him may not perish but may have eternal life" (John 3:16). In Matthew's portrayal of the Last Judgment based on helping the needy, the Lord says that the just will go off to "eternal life" (Matt 25:31–46). And writing to the Romans, Paul says, "The wages of sin is death, but the free gift of God is eternal life in Christ Jesus our Lord" (Rom 6:23), and to the Galatians that a person who sows to the Spirit will "reap eternal life" (Gal 6:8).

Christian tradition calls sharing the eternal life of Christ "heaven" and describes it in various ways, including the "Father's house," the "heavenly Jerusalem," and a "paradise" of happiness. In heaven, the faithful enjoy the "beatific" vision, the contemplation of God's eternal glory. They are forever united with Christ and with all the saved in the communion of saints.

Saint Paul reminds us of our essential human limitations in imagining what heaven is like: "What no eye has seen, nor ear heard, nor the human heart conceived, what God has prepared for those who love him" (1 Cor 2:9). We cannot describe heaven as it is because eternal life is not governed by our time-space dimensions. There are no calendars or clocks and no distances or measurements in heaven. Eternity is not a very long time that poses a problem of boredom. Nor does it make sense to try to figure out where we spend eternity. We can think of eternal life as the fulfillment of time, the reward of time well spent, the free, unmerited gift of sharing in God's everlasting life. We can speak of heaven as the ultimate fulfillment of the deepest longings of our hearts and imagine a life of complete happiness, where there is no more sorrow, pain, or tears.

Thanks to the salvation optimism taught by Vatican II—that God's saving grace is available to all who follow their conscience—we can hope that our deceased loved ones are in the gracious hands of the God who wills the salvation of all people (see 1 Tim 2:4).

Throughout history, Christians have expressed their belief in life everlasting in two distinct ways: the "resurrection of the body," as found in the biblical tradition and the Apostles' Creed; and the "immortality of the soul," rooted in Greek philosophy and affirmed in popular piety today. Each approach reminds us of important truths: we are inspirited bodies that are temples of the

Holy Spirit and worthy of respect. Our bodily existence is graced and destined for everlasting life as members of the Body of Christ.

At the same time, we are embodied spirits that transcend the limits of the material world. We work out our salvation by a proper use of our intelligence and free will. We survive death and enjoy everlasting life in union with God, the inexhaustible Mystery. In sum, we look forward to the "life of the world to come," where, as whole persons—body and soul—we enjoy a happiness beyond comprehension, in union with Christ and the vast throng of saints praising God forever.

*How can belief in heaven help us persevere in doing good even when we achieve little progress?*

# 3

## The Virtues

The *Catechism* teaches,

> Virtue is a habitual and firm disposition to do good. The human virtues are stable dispositions of the intellect and the will that govern our acts, order our passions, and guide our conduct in accordance with reason and faith. They can be grouped around the four cardinal virtues: prudence, justice, fortitude, and temperance. Prudence disposes the practical reason to discern, in every circumstance, our true good and to choose the right means for achieving it. Justice consists in the firm and constant will to give God and neighbor their due. Fortitude ensures firmness in difficulties and constancy in the pursuit of the good. Temperance moderates the attraction of the pleasures of the senses and provides balance in the use of created goods. The moral virtues grow through education, deliberate acts, and perseverance in struggle. Divine grace purifies and elevates them.
>
> The theological virtues dispose Christians to live in a relationship with the Holy Trinity. They have God for their

origin, their motive, and their object—God known by faith, God hoped in and loved for his own sake. There are three theological virtues: faith, hope, and charity. They inform all the moral virtues and give life to them. By faith, we believe in God and believe all that he has revealed to us and that Holy Church proposes for our belief. By hope we desire, and with steadfast trust await from God, eternal life and the graces to merit it. By charity, we love God above all things and our neighbor as ourselves for love of God. Charity, the form of all virtues, "binds everything together in perfect harmony" (Col 3:14).[1]

# THEOLOGICAL VIRTUES

## Faith

In his classic treatment of the virtues, Thomas Aquinas (1225–1274) identifies three scripture-based theological virtues, faith, hope, and charity (see 1 Cor 13:13)—free gifts that direct us to a proper relationship to God. Aquinas argues that faith is the first among the virtues because we cannot love or hope for what we do not know. Following Augustine—his primary theological source—Aquinas says that "believing is giving assent to something we are still thinking about." As Christians, our fundamental belief is that God loves us and rewards those who seek him, as is revealed in sacred scripture and specified in the traditional creeds. Faith is a "mental disposition" or an act of the mind that accepts what God has revealed because God is totally trustworthy. Over time, the nuanced Thomistic emphasis on the cognitive aspect of faith degenerated into a "propositional" understanding of faith and revelation that focused more on accepting Church doctrines

---

1.  *Catechism of the Catholic Church* §§1833–44.

than living the Christian faith. Good Catholics had faith in the official teachings of the Church, obscure as they might seem.

The Second Vatican Council (1962–1965), reflecting theological developments of the twentieth century, retrieved a more biblical, personal, and relational notion of Christian faith. In the Hebrew scriptures, Abraham and Sarah are the great examples of faith, because they trusted God's promise and totally surrendered themselves to God's will by leaving their homeland without knowing their destination. In the New Testament, the Gospel of John roots faith in a personal encounter with Jesus, who is himself the Word of God and the source of eternal life. The Apostle Paul insists that we are saved not by performing the works of the law, but by faith in God's grace revealed in Christ Jesus.

As a result of God's free, unmerited self-communication, we participate in the divine life. Through the gift of faith, we have the capacity to say yes to God our Father, to commit ourselves to Christ our Savior, and to follow the promptings of the Holy Spirit our Advocate. From that personalistic perspective, Church dogmas appear not as the object of faith but as expressions of community belief that elucidate various aspects of our relationship to God. Christian faith involves both the heart and the head, both loving commitment and deeper awareness.

Drawing on influential theologians, especially Karl Rahner, we can distinguish "faith" as a positive existential stance from "belief" as a personal appropriation of a particular Christian teaching. Some examples can make that abstract distinction clearer and indicate its significance for our spiritual lives. Bill, who is sometimes overwhelmed by the absurdity of such immense human suffering in the world, still thinks, against all logic, that human existence is meaningful, and that life makes sense. He finds support for this faith in the Christian belief in the resurrection of Jesus, an innocent victim who took on the sufferings of the world and was raised to a new and victorious life.

Jill, who suffers from an abiding sense of unworthiness, of not measuring up, is surprised and grateful that she feels loved somewhere deep in her soul. She relates this gift of faith to the Christian belief that God is a merciful Father who embraces all human beings with an unconditional divinizing love.

*What is my own fundamental faith conviction and Christian belief and how can they illumine my spiritual journey in today's complex world?*

## Hope

According to Thomas Aquinas, the theological virtue of hope inclines us to seek our highest goal, eternal life with God, and to rely confidently on divine assistance to attain it. With hope we can also discern and seek other goals, difficult but attainable, that can further our primary goal of union with God.

We can read the Hebrew scriptures as a grand narrative of human hope inspired by a series of promises made by God to the great Israelite leaders, Moses and David, and to the major prophets, Isaiah and Jeremiah, who assured the Israelites that hope for an ideal leader to establish justice and peace would one day be fulfilled. The New Testament proclaims that Jesus fulfilled this promise, not as a worldly king, but as a suffering servant who died on the cross, was raised to life, and will one day complete his saving mission.

Throughout history, the Christian tradition has, at times, put so much emphasis on the hope for everlasting happiness with God that it has neglected concern for the well-being of this world, which has drawn the Marxist criticism that religion functions like an opiate. We find that attitude today among Catholics who go to Mass regularly to stay on good terms with the "Man Upstairs" but automatically tune out homilies that talk about creating a more just world. In dialogue with Marxists, theologians have developed a contemporary theology of hope that uses the hope for heaven as a catalyst for spreading the kingdom of peace and justice in this world. There is a synergistic relationship between hoping for heaven and hoping for a more humane earthly home. Confident of God's help, hope encourages us to make our world a better place. Progress in the struggle against evil strengthens our hope in the final triumph of good.

Joe and Mary, both practicing Catholics, were having serious marital problems, intensified after their three children were out on their own. Life was pretty miserable, and they were about to file for divorce until they were both struck by a homily at Mass that emphasized that in difficult situations we should not give up hope because with God all things are possible. They talked about their situation with their pastor who said that, as things stand, it certainly did not make sense to stay together and that the only way to save the marriage was to imagine a better relationship, to envision pleasing one another, and to hope for a happy future together. He suggested they stop the harsh attacks, spend weekends doing things they both enjoy, and pray together for God's help. The good news is that over time their hopes were fulfilled, and they have made a better, mutually enriching marriage. This happy development has deepened their confidence in God's grace and prompted them to share their experience with engaged couples in their parish marriage preparation program.

*How can my hope to get to heaven strengthen my commitment to make the world a better place?*

# Charity

Thomas Aquinas defines the theological virtue of charity as an unmerited gift from God that enables us to live in friendship with God, to participate in the life of the Trinity, and to experience something of eternal beatitude while still on earth. As scripture teaches us, God has first loved us, which enables us to love (see 1 John 4:19). Our friendship with the triune God, who always loves us steadfastly and unconditionally, is dynamic, always open to further growth and development. Lukewarm believers can fall in love with God, nominal Christians can develop a relationship with Christ, and good Catholics can get more energized by the Holy Spirit.

Recognizing our limitations as lovers can function positively, preserving us from self-righteousness and encouraging us to deepen our love for God. Furthermore, the ever-merciful God can transform our sinful failures to love into more effective exercises of the virtue of charity. The God proclaimed by Christ is not a stern judge but a passionate lover who seeks to befriend us. Through the gift of grace, we can return that love, at least in some measure, and to delight in the gift of friendship with God.

The virtue of charity inclines us not only to love God but also to love our neighbor. These two loves are essentially united so that they necessarily interact in an authentic Christian life. John states in his first letter, "Those who say, 'I love God,' and hate their brothers or sisters, are liars" (1 John 4:20). We are called to love our neighbors because they also are loved by God and share in the gift of divine friendship. God's love excludes no one and embraces all human beings, creating a universal fellowship, an all-inclusive community of love. The virtue of charity empowers us to do the hard work of maintaining healthy family relationships, to set aside our own needs to meet the needs of our friends, and to get along with troublesome colleagues at work. As Jesus teaches through word and example, charity also prompts us to expand our circle of love to include those in need, the poor, the vulnerable, and even our enemies. Charity is true to itself when it is prepared to give more tomorrow than today and when it is ready to sacrifice self to serve others.

Individuals practice charity in various ways. Tim expresses his love for God by going to Mass a couple of times during the week. Mary practiced tough love by enrolling her drug-addicted teenage son into a drug rehab program. Sam deepens his loving relationship with his wife by regularly paying her honest compliments. Martha cares for her elderly neighbor by doing grocery shopping for her. Don helped create a better work environment by befriending a Black coworker. Sylvia got her friend through a tough divorce by being a good listener. Jose helps the poor by serving meals once a week at a food distribution center. Sharon gave up a very lucrative job to become a community organizer in the inner city.

*How can you practice the virtue of charity in a world that rewards selfishness?*

# CARDINAL VIRTUES

## Prudence

Following the Roman philosopher Cicero, Thomas Aquinas lists prudence as one of the cardinal or principal virtues along with justice, fortitude, and temperance. Aquinas borrows definitions of prudence from his two most influential sources: Aristotle, who said that "prudence is right reason applied to action," and Augustine, who described prudence as "love discerning aright that which helps from that which hinders us in tending to God." Prudence is a virtue, a stable habit that enables us to make good decisions about what we should do in various situations and moves us to act on this insight. Much like a properly formed conscience, it identifies the fitting thing to do in diverse circumstances and then empowers us to take the proper course of action.

For Christians, prudence is a gift of God, a product of an unmerited grace that divinizes us and empowers us to do God's will, to follow Christ, and to listen to the Holy Spirit. Charity, the greatest of all the virtues, enables us to live in friendship with God and to spread the reign of God in the world. Prudence, the "mother" of the cardinal virtues, prompts us to follow the best means to achieve our life goal of union with God.

The gift of prudence, which is given freely, enlightens our mind and strengthens our will. It requires our cooperation to develop and apply it. We become more prudent persons by attending to our expanding experience and by remembering what increases our Christian commitment and what diminishes it. We do not expect teenagers with little experience to have a highly developed sense of prudence. We do, however, hope that, as we grow older, we become more prudent.

We grow in prudence by understanding ourselves better, by a more accurate assessment of our strengths and weaknesses, and by distinguishing which of our instinctive reactions we can trust from those that lead us astray. Regular self-examination is a valuable spiritual exercise for developing the virtue of prudence. We also need to become more adept at reading situations, understanding the dynamics of complex circumstances, and foreseeing consequences of our actions, both intended and unintended. Prudent persons avoid the extreme of rash behavior, acting too quickly without really appreciating the nuances and the complexities of the situation. They also avoid the other extreme of temporizing or procrastination, delaying required action, overthinking the problem, and looking for the perfect solution, all of which preclude pursuing a reasonable and good solution.

Consider, for example, a father who began by raising his only son in much the same way that he was raised, with strict discipline, harsh punishments, and emotional distance—an imprudent approach that left him with an angry, rebellious teenager disrupting family life. Following suggestions from his pastor and guidance from his wife, he worked diligently at becoming a more prudent father. He came to understand that his role as a Christian father is not to produce a clone or an obedient kid but to cooperate with God's grace in helping his son become a free and responsible adult. To promote this goal, he adopted various prudent strategies: recognizing and managing his own perfectionist tendencies inherited from his father; expressing, in word as well as deed, his genuine love for his son; listening more to him as a way of bolstering his self-esteem and learning more about him and his very different world; and praying his son develops his God-given gifts and talents. This strategy bore fruit during the pandemic, as he enjoyed many amiable conversations with his collegiate son, who was living back at home while the university was closed. This set the stage for a mutually rewarding relationship with his son.

*How can I become a more prudent person in our complex world?*

# Justice

## *Interpersonal Justice*

Following Aristotle, Thomas Aquinas defined justice as "the strong and firm will to give to each his due"[2] and described its function as establishing a proper order among things. We could say that the virtue of justice inclines us to act fairly, to respect the rights of others, and to seek a reasonable equity among human beings. It attunes us to injustice and inequity. Consider, for example, that women are paid less than men for comparable work and that Hispanics make less than whites for similar jobs. The more we become aware of injustices in our world, the more we realize the importance of cultivating the virtue of justice.

The fact that human beings possess certain rights grounds the obligation to promote justice by respecting and ensuring their rights. Some rights are natural because they are based on

---

2. St. Thomas Aquinas, *STh* II-II, 47, 2.

the fundamental nature of human existence. As theists, we believe that human beings have certain rights because they are children of God, made in the divine image—for example, the right to be treated with respect and to be included in community life. This means, however, that we have a moral obligation to oppose racial discrimination and to support inclusive communities.

Aquinas distinguishes various types of justice, including what he calls "commutative justice" and what we might name "interpersonal justice," which fosters equitable exchanges among individuals and groups—what is due to the other is determined by convention, by oral agreement, or by contract. For example, a godfather meets his obligation to his godson by giving him an annual birthday present, as is the custom in his family. A homeowner acts justly by paying a student to cut her grass the agreed amount, and the student practices justice by doing a good job. An electrician pays his just dues to his union, which in turn helps protect his right to fair wages and safe working conditions. Just persons strive to interact with others in ways that are fair and equitable.

As Christians, we recognize that justice should be informed, guided, and expanded by charity. Justice inclines us to do the minimum to fulfill our obligation to others and to meet their needs. Charity inclines us to go the extra mile, to go beyond merely meeting our obligations, and to be extra generous in responding to the needs of others. We can imagine, for example, the godfather, who becomes a needed mentor and confidant to his teenage godson; the homeowner, who gives a generous bonus to the student who tends her lawn; and the electrician, who does a lot of *pro bono* work for family and friends. Justice gives what is due; charity gives without calculating the cost.

*What specific steps can I take to become more just in a society diminished by inequities?*

## *Distributive Justice*

Thomas Aquinas, who built his whole moral theology on the foundation of the virtues, distinguished the justice that governs interpersonal exchanges from distributive justice that guides political leaders to create an equitable society. Just rulers distribute "resources in proper proportion," giving to each what their situation requires and deserves. They must consider the common good as well as the needs of those with competing interests. Their primary responsibility is to promote and guide a just society.

In a modern democracy like the United States, all citizens can practice the virtue of distributive justice in the ongoing effort to create a more equitable society. We believe in a "government of the people, by the people, for the people," as Lincoln put it in his memorable Gettysburg Address. As citizens, we can influence distribution policies by voting for candidates committed to proportionate justice and by supporting just approaches to public policy issues, such as minimum wage, welfare benefits, and taxation reform. Public opinion does not always prevail against special interest groups, but it does influence legislation.

In addressing issues of distributive justice, Catholic Social Teaching begins with the principle of "the universal destination of goods," which asserts that "God gave the earth to the whole human race for the sustenance of all its members, without excluding or favoring anyone" (*Laudato Si'* 93). Individuals have a right to own private property, but that is subordinated to the right of all persons to the goods of this earth necessary for a decent standard of living.

In the United States, statistical studies consistently show great wealth disparity between the very rich few and most Americans. For example, the top 1 percent of Americans possess over 40 percent of the total wealth in the United States, while the lower 50 percent have just over 1 percent.[3] The four hundred richest Americans have more wealth than 21 million minority households. Some economists argue that this inequality poses a threat to our economy and our democracy. The American Catholic bishops view it as a violation of distributive justice that calls for remedial actions.

Closing this wealth gap is a complex problem and admits of no swift or easy solutions. The virtue of distributive justice inclines us to do what we can: paying our fair share of taxes; recognizing that inequality can hurt the affluent as well as the poor; empowering the poor to take charge of their own lives; supporting policies that reflect the "preferential option for the poor" enunciated by Catholic Social Teaching; voting for candidates who favor closing the wage and wealth gap; and praying with the prophet Amos that justice will descend on our land like a mighty stream (see Amos 5:24).

*How can I practice the virtue of distributive justice in our politically polarized society?*

## *Social Justice*

In his treatment of justice, Thomas Aquinas, following Aristotle, distinguishes three types: commutative, distributive, and legal or general justice, which provides norms governing social interactions serving the common good. In the twentieth century, popes, scholars, and activists, concerned that the term *legal* narrowed justice to keeping laws, began to speak about the importance of *social justice,* a broader term that has become common in Catholic social thought.

In the United States, Catholic immigrants contributed to social justice by overcoming the Nativist (anti-Catholic) prejudice

---

3. See "The Distribution of Wealth in the United States and Implications for a Net Worth Tax," Washington Center for Equitable Growth, March 21, 2019, https://equitablegrowth.org.

and moving into the mainstream of American life, especially through electoral politics and organized labor. By far, the most important individual advocate for social justice was Dorothy Day (1897–1980), a journalist and social activist, who learned about Catholic social thought from a French peasant, Peter Maurin. Together with him, Day started publishing on May 1, 1922, the monthly newspaper, *The Catholic Worker*, which gave her a lifetime forum for applying Catholic Social Teaching to current issues. For example, she argued for the right of workers to unionize (she battled Cardinal Spellman over the right of grave diggers to form a union), supported child labor laws, and defended the civil rights movement. She consistently spoke out against all wars, including World War II and Vietnam, and vigorously opposed all forms of discrimination, including racism, sexism, and anti-Semitism. Day gave witness to social justice not only by word but also by deed, as she participated in rallies, demonstrations, marches, and acts of civil disobedience that often landed her in jail. Dorothy Day reminds us of what the virtue of social justice looks like in practice.

Official Church teaching eventually caught up with the witness to justice of faithful Catholics. In 1937, Pope Pius XI declared that the essence of social justice is "to demand from individuals everything necessary for the common good" (*Divini Redemptoris* 51) and said its function is to penetrate all the "institutions of social life" (see *Quadragesimo Anno* 88). Building on the Second Vatican Council, the 1971 Synod of Bishops made one of the most significant statements about social justice: "Action on behalf of justice and transformation of the world fully appear to us as a constitutive dimension of the preaching of the Gospel."

During his long pontificate, Pope John Paul II often invoked norms of social justice to deal with a range of issues: for example, respect for human rights, solidarity with workers, the need to empower the poor, cooperative international relationships, the proper use of political power, and promoting the common good. Echoing this broad understanding of social justice, Pope Francis has put special emphasis on the systemic causes of poverty and the gospel call to care for persons in need.

Imagine a woman who, inspired by Dorothy Day's autobiography, *The Long Loneliness*, is trying to develop the virtue of social justice. She listens to the Sunday readings for inspired passages on working for justice; decides to concentrate on the problem of racism in her neighborhood; reads a couple of articles on the root causes of the problem; joins the parish social justice committee, which institutes a series of dialogues between Black, Hispanic, and white parishioners; befriends an African American neighbor; and prays regularly for racial harmony.

*How can I practice the virtue of social justice in our society that struggles with systemic injustice?*

# Fortitude

According to Aquinas, the cardinal virtue of fortitude helps us deal with our fears in effective ways so that we are neither too timid nor too rash. It enables us to face serious challenges, even death, with a measure of calm; to endure suffering for a just cause; and to work courageously on behalf of the good. Our personal fears have a distinctive countenance but enough family resemblance so we can recognize something of the fears that alarm and disquiet others. During the pandemic, some fears of the virus were useful and constructive, for example, prompting people to take proper precautions. Other fears were limiting and restrictive, for example, moving people to forego safe practices like walking alone outside. Some fears were generated by real probabilities, such as the fact that the pandemic would adversely impact the economy; other fears proved to be illusory, such as the one that the pandemic meant the imminent end of the world.

For some people, the isolation demanded by COVID-19 produced not a specific fear of a particular threat but a general anxiety that is hard to identify and describe, such as a vague sense that something important is not right, that we are radically vulnerable, that we are alone in the struggle against the dark forces, and that death is the last word.

In the face of fears and anxieties, Christian fortitude draws on the biblical tradition. In the Book of Isaiah, Yahweh tells the Israelites, "Do not fear, for I am with you, do not be afraid, for I am your God" (Isa 41:10). The Psalmist has provided countless believers with a comforting image: "Even though I walk through the darkest valley, I fear no evil; for you are with me; your rod and your staff—they comfort me" (Ps 23:4). This theme reappears in the New Testament. When the angel Gabriel appeared to Mary, he encouraged her not to be afraid (see Luke 1:30). When a sudden storm threatened the lives of the fishermen disciples of Jesus, he said to them, "'Why are you afraid, you of little faith?' Then he got up and rebuked the winds and the sea; and there was a dead calm" (Matt 8:24–26). During his agony in the garden, Jesus reinforced his teaching by courageously overcoming his own trepidation over his pending "cup of suffering" and submitting himself once again to God's will (see Matt 26:42).

As Christians, we are called to follow the example of Jesus by rising above what troubles us, by acting courageously despite our anxieties, and by living a life of freedom rather than fear.

*How can I develop, with God's help, the virtue of fortitude so that I can rise above my personal fears and anxieties?*

# Temperance

Following tradition, Thomas Aquinas listed temperance as the fourth cardinal virtue after prudence, justice, and fortitude.

He saw it as the virtue that enables us to manage reasonably our strong physical desires, especially for food, drink, and sex.

In the United States, the word *temperance* came to be associated primarily with the control of alcohol. The Temperance Movement, which viewed the consumption of alcoholic beverages as sinful and the source of widespread social evil, succeeded in passing the 1920 Eighteenth Amendment prohibiting the manufacture, sale, and distribution of alcoholic beverages. This socially disastrous legislation, repealed in 1933 by the Twenty-First Amendment, associated temperance with an unenlightened attempt to control something not necessarily evil.

We need to recover a more balanced and nuanced understanding of the virtue of temperance. God's creation possesses a fundamental goodness and should be treated with respect. God's grace has created human beings as inspirited bodies with life-preserving desires for food, drink, and sex that share in the essential goodness of creation. We deal effectively with our desires not by disparaging bodily pleasures as tainted by evil but by developing a proper self-control that incorporates them into a wholesome life-giving friendship with God. The Temperance Movement demonized all alcohol consumption. Puritanism, in its Catholic and Protestant versions, fosters negative attitudes toward human sexuality. Authentic Christian temperance refuses to demonize or disparage God's creation.

The virtue of temperance inclines us to order our desires for pleasure so that we become more fully human, more integrated persons, and more dedicated to serving God. Truly temperate persons manage their desires with a certain inner serenity, a calm confidence that with God's help they can act reasonably in diverse circumstances. They can enjoy a good dinner without overeating and have a drink or two at a party without worry of excess. Temperate spouses spontaneously try to please their partners in their lovemaking.

Inner serenity is a gift of God, an unmerited blessing, but it calls for our cooperation to solidify and expand it. The Christian tradition of voluntary fasting can be part of an overall effort to develop better eating patterns. Doing the twelve-step program of Alcoholics Anonymous can be helpful in dealing with addiction to alcohol. Honest conversation between spouses about sexual desires and needs can lead to more satisfying lovemaking. The virtue of temperance does not disparage bodily pleasures but enlists them in living a full Christian life.

*How can the cardinal virtue of temperance help me manage the temptations of the contemporary world?*

# TRUTHFULNESS

## In Personal Relationships

According to the classic moral theology of Thomas Aquinas, the virtue of truthfulness inclines us to present ourselves in "both life and speech" as we really are — "neither greater nor less" than we really are. In other words, we are called to avoid a false pride that inflates our importance and accomplishments as well as a false humility that undervalues our true worth.

For Aquinas, truthfulness is allied with the virtue of justice, based on the notion that others have a right to hear the truth from us and that we have a corresponding duty to act and speak truthfully in our personal interactions. Critics of this approach contend that it contributes to a legalistic and minimalistic approach to truth telling with emphasis on how much of our truth we must share with others and what can we withhold without being guilty of lying.

When charity informs and guides our practice of truthfulness, however, this virtue moves us to develop deeper, richer, healthier, and more satisfying personal relationships. Honest and fitting communication are an expression of love of neighbor. Charity and not frankness guides us in how much of our truth we share with others. Deciding what to share with family and friends considers their strengths and weaknesses, as well as their potential for growth and their vulnerability. In general, we can ask ourselves if disclosure helps or harms the relationship or if it diminishes or increases mutual love. Common wisdom declares honesty is the best policy, but sometimes prudent nondisclosure is the more charitable option. The sharing of hidden thoughts and feelings can facilitate more honest conversations and deepen mutual love, but, in some situations, it can be harmful and ought to be avoided. Interpersonal truthfulness is not only informed by charity but also guided by prudence.

Positive, effective exercises of the virtue of truthfulness can be seen in family relationships. A husband in a tolerable marriage, for example, found it gradually improved when his wife responded positively to his disclosure of his need for more sexual intimacy. A wife, who finally got the courage to tell her husband honestly how frustrated she gets when he interrupts her in conversations with their friends, was pleasantly surprised that he now tries to be more respectful. A father, who was often critical of his rebellious teenage son, followed his wife's advice and started paying him honest compliments, which led to a healthier relationship. A married man, who recognized his need for help to keep his friendship with a single female friend from becoming inappropriate, decided to protect himself from his own libido not by hinting at a potential problem to his wife, but by telling the whole story to his pastor, who offered helpful spiritual guidance. A grandmother revealed her own youthful struggles and transgressions to her collegiate granddaughter, hoping it would help her deal with her own personal challenges. A troubled woman in her late twenties, who suddenly remembered she was sexually abused by her father in her youth, decided to confront him as part of her therapy, but not to tell her mother, who would be devastated.

*How can I practice the virtue of truthfulness in my personal relationships?*

# In Public Life

The virtue of truthfulness is not only crucial to healthy personal relationships but also in carrying out our vocation to extend the reign of God in the world. Truth is central to the Christian tradition. For Christians, God is Absolute Truth, the Source of all truth and the Goal of all truth seeking. Jesus Christ, the Word made flesh, is Truth incarnate, the definitive manifestation of divine truth, "the way, and the truth, and the life" (John 14:6). In word and deed, he proclaimed the truth that sets us free (see John 8:32) and taught us the way of truthful living. As promised, Christ sent the Holy Spirit, the Paraclete, the Spirit of Truth, to help us understand and practice his fundamental teachings. Empowered by the Spirit, the Church is the community called to bear witness to the truth, to be an authentic sign and instrument of the kingdom, and to keep alive the memory of Jesus, who spoke the truth to the powerful and those who are marginalized. Prayer—both liturgical and private—is a form of truth telling that expresses the fundamental truth that we are totally dependent on the God who loves and forgives us. Christian morality is not primarily about keeping laws but about honestly and generously living Christ's command to love our neighbor as ourselves.

Prayerful reflection can reveal deceitful tendencies that impede and limit our ability to serve the kingdom. There is the temptation to think of our talents as personal possessions to be used for our own benefit rather than free gifts of the Spirit given for the benefit of others and for the common good. Some people tend to undervalue their gifts, thinking they have nothing to offer to make the world a better place. Others tend to exaggerate their own importance and talents, making it difficult to cooperate with others on worthy causes. There is a brand of Christian piety that concentrates so much on getting to heaven that it neglects the responsibility to spread the reign of truth, justice, and peace in this world.

Catholic Social Teaching insists that serving the kingdom of God requires a careful reading of the "signs of the time," accurate assessments of societal dynamics, and honest judgments of the most effective means for promoting the common good. By matching an honest discernment of our gifts with an accurate assessment of societal needs, we can discern concrete ways of making the world a better place and serving the common good.

Young people, for example, who have learned scientific facts about the dangers of global warming, could join an activist group like Citizens' Climate Lobby (CCL) that promotes bipartisan conversations with elected officials on controlling carbon emissions. A successful executive, who always took for granted the advantages of growing up in an affluent family, could recognize the truth of her privileged life and commit herself to helping the less fortunate. A priest could commit himself to include more of the Church's social teaching in his homilies after admitting to himself the harsh truth that he muted that teaching for fear of offending his parishioners and losing their financial support.

*How can the virtue of truthfulness prompt me to use my gifts to spread the kingdom and serve the common good in our post-truth culture?*

# 4

## The Gifts of the Holy Spirit

The *Catechism* teaches,

The seven gifts of the Holy Spirit are wisdom, understanding, counsel, fortitude, knowledge, piety, and fear of the Lord. As Christians, we walk with the seven gifts of the Holy Spirit. Wisdom enables us to see the world from God's viewpoint, which can help us come to grasp the purpose and plan of God. It grants us the long-range view of history, examining the present in the light of the past and the mystery of the future. It saves us from the illusion that the spirit of the times is our only guide. The Spirit's gift of knowledge directs us to contemplation, or thoughtful reflection of the mystery of God—Father, Son, and Holy Spirit—as well as the mysteries of the Catholic faith. We are drawn to meditative prayer, where we allow God to lead us while we rest patiently in the divine presence.[1]

# WISDOM

There is a long tradition in the Christian world of reflection on the seven gifts of the Holy Spirit, commonly identified as wisdom, understanding, counsel, fortitude, knowledge, piety, and fear of the Lord. The prophet Isaiah declared that the promised Messiah would possess gifts of the Spirit: "The spirit of the LORD shall rest on him, the spirit of wisdom and understanding, the spirit of counsel and might, the spirit of knowledge and the fear of the LORD" (Isa 11:1–3). An influential Greek translation added "piety," making seven gifts, a number suggesting perfection and plenitude.

The Hebrew scriptures praise King Solomon for asking God for the gift of wisdom and exercising it throughout his long reign. For example, he solved the dispute between two women claiming to be the mother of a baby by suggesting they cut the infant in half, a solution rejected by the real mother (see 1 Kgs 3:16–28). The New Testament presents Jesus as greater than Solomon (see Matt 12:42), the very wisdom of God (see 1 Cor 1:24), the wise teacher who reveals the secrets of the Father (see John 15:15) and shares the gift of wisdom with us.

In his *Summa Theologiae*, Thomas Aquinas affirms the traditional teaching that the gift of wisdom "strengthens the mind in the hope and certainty of eternal things." The wise person keeps things in perspective, takes the long view, maintains hope in God's plan to bring all things to perfection. According to Aquinas,

---

1. *United States Catechism for Adults* (Washington, DC: USCCB, 2006), 208–9; see also *Catechism of the Catholic Church*, §§1831–32.

the gift of wisdom is a habit that inclines us to follow the promptings of the Spirit when faced with difficult decisions.

In 2014, Pope Francis gave a series of catechetical instructions on the gifts of the Holy Spirit. Beginning with the gift of wisdom, he noted the example of Solomon and described wisdom as the "grace of being able to see everything with the eyes of God." Wisdom teaches us to "feel with God's heart, to speak with God's words." It gives us a "taste and savor for God," enabling us to discern when "something is of God and when it is not of God." Recognizing the temptation to see the world with a disordered heart and biased mind, the pope urges us to pray for the gift of wisdom so that we can go forth to spread the reign of God in our families and our world.

Recently, the directors of a homeless shelter were faced with a problem. Three young men on a couple of occasions came into the shelter drunk and caused trouble. Should they be banned permanently from the shelter, putting them out on the streets? Should they be allowed in to disrupt the sleep of the other guests? The directors decided that the three men seeking entry would have to pass a breathalyzer test. If they had a blood alcohol level over 0.08, they would be denied entry for one night. If they failed two tests in a row, they would be denied entry for a week. No one else seeking entry would have to take a test, because the shelter welcomes drinkers provided they do not cause trouble. The three young men, when consulted, thought the rules were acceptable and signed a contract agreeing to them. Eyes of faith can detect the Spirit of wisdom at work in this decision that respects the rights of nondisruptive guests in the shelter and allows the troublesome ones to decide their own fate on any given night.

*How can I deal more wisely with the challenges of our world today?*

# UNDERSTANDING

The seven gifts of the Holy Spirit play a prominent role in the sacrament of confirmation. After asking the congregation to pray for those to be confirmed, the bishop prays,

> Almighty God, Father of our Lord Jesus Christ,
> who brought these servants to new birth
> by water and the Holy Spirit,
> freeing them from sin:
> send upon them, O Lord, the Holy Spirit, the
> Paraclete;
> give them the spirit of wisdom and understanding,
> the spirit of counsel and fortitude,
> the spirit of knowledge and piety;
> fill them with the spirit of fear of the Lord.
> Through Christ our Lord.

Thomas Aquinas notes that the gift of "understanding" enables us to penetrate eternal realities in themselves and to recognize divine truth as the ideal for the full Christian life. This gift enables us to understand both the deepest longings of our heart for eternal life and the means needed to attain it.

As part of a series of catechetical instructions on the seven gifts of the Holy Spirit, Pope Francis taught that the gift of understanding "awakens" in us the "ability to go beyond the outward appearance of reality and to probe the depths of the thoughts of God and his plan of salvation."[2] The pope gives understanding perspective by citing the apostle Paul: "What no eye has seen, nor ear heard, nor the human heart conceived, what God has prepared for those who love him" (1 Cor 2:9–10). This does not mean we

---

2. Pope Francis, General Audience, April 30, 2014, www.vatican.va.

can "have full knowledge of the designs of God" as we walk this earth. It is true, however, that Christ has sent us the Holy Spirit, who helps us understand our "situation in depth" and who introduces us "into intimacy with God." The Spirit, who dwells within us, helps us "grow daily" in our understanding all that Jesus taught us and enables us "to read inwardly" the depths of God's words.

As an example of the depth and power of the gift of understanding, Francis recounted the story of Cleopas and his companion fleeing from Jerusalem to Emmaus after the death of Jesus. The risen Christ joins them on their journey, but "their eyes, veiled with sadness and despair, are unable to recognize him." When, however, Jesus explains the scriptures to them and breaks bread with them, "their minds are opened and hope is rekindled in their hearts" (see Luke 24:13–27). The pope encourages us to ask for the gift of understanding, which opens our minds "to understand better the things of God, human things, situations, all things."[3]

Chris and Connie, a middle-aged couple in a troubled marriage, were both struck by a homily at Sunday Mass that encouraged marriage partners to think of ways they could be good for one another: staying in good physical condition, keeping intellectually stimulated, satisfying emotional needs, and growing together spiritually. They both intuitively understood the potential of this positive proactive approach to their marriage and decided to start with the physical by taking walks together whenever possible.

*How can the gift of understanding help me manage the complexities of our rapidly changing world?*

# COUNSEL

In the farewell discourse in John's Gospel, Jesus promises, "And I will ask the Father, and he will give you another Advocate,

---

3. Pope Francis, General Audience, April 30, 2014, www.vatican.va.

to be with you forever. This is the Spirit of truth" (John 14:16–17). Jesus goes on: "But the Advocate, the Holy Spirit, whom the Father will send in my name, will teach you everything, and remind you of all that I have said to you" (14:26). The Greek word commonly translated as "Advocate" or "Paraclete" refers to a person called to the side of one in need of assistance. In John's Gospel it has the broad meaning of a "helper" and is translated as "advocate." We can think of the Spirit as our counselor, who bears witness to Jesus (see John 15:26) and alerts us to destructive cultural trends and societal sins (see John 16:6–11).

Thomas Aquinas taught that we need the guidance of the Holy Spirit and the gift of "counsel" to make good decisions because of our own limitations and the complexity of our circumstances, surely multiplied in our post-pandemic world. Counsel, which perfects the cardinal virtue of prudence, helps us to follow God's will in our everyday life, which can be complicated, complex, and confusing.

On May 7, 2014, Pope Francis spoke on the gift of the Holy Spirit traditionally known as "counsel."[4] After quoting the Psalmist, "I bless the LORD who gives me counsel; in the night also my heart instructs me" (Ps 16:7), the pope noted how much, in delicate situations, we "count on the advice of people who are wise and who love us." As Christians, we believe that we have an even greater divine gift that "enlightens our heart so as to make us understand the right way to speak and to behave and the way to follow." The Spirit inspires us "to turn our interior gaze to Jesus" as our model for relating with God and our neighbor. The gift of counsel enables us to overcome self-centered ways and to make concrete choices "in communion with God, according to the logic of Jesus and his Gospel." Francis encourages us to stay faithful to

---

4. Pope Francis, General Audience, May 7, 2014, www.vatican.va.

prayer so that a "deep, almost connatural harmony in the Spirit" grows and develops within us, enabling us to put on the mind of Christ.

The Holy Spirit speaks to us not only in the "intimacy of the heart" but also through the "voice and witness" of the "whole Christian community." It is a great gift to encounter men and women of faith who, at crucial times in our lives, "help us to bring light to our heart and to recognize the Lord's will!"[5]

For example, Ellie, a married woman with one child, is a committed Catholic with deep spiritual sensibilities. She was distressed that Sue, her longtime friend and spiritual soulmate, was about to get engaged to Bill, a guy she knew very well and thought would be a poor match for Sue. Relying on the guidance of the Holy Spirit, she asked Sue if they could talk about her pending engagement. After they prayed together, Ellie went over a list of things that troubled her about Bill: he often interrupts women in conversation; he talks a lot about himself; he has not been to Mass in years, not even on Christmas or Easter; he has no good male friends; he becomes aggressive when drinking; he lives above his financial means; and he is very influenced by his father, who tends to be sexist in his opinions.

Getting beyond her initial defensiveness, Sue discussed each point, rejecting some and taking others seriously. Ellie and Sue ended their conversation as they began, with a prayer asking for guidance from the Holy Spirit. About a month later, Sue told Ellie that she had broken off the relationship and was feeling very peaceful with her decision.

*Do I have a spiritual director or confidant to accompany me on my spiritual journey?*

---

5. Pope Francis, General Audience, May 7, 2014, www.vatican.va.

# FORTITUDE

The sequence for Pentecost Sunday, "Come, Holy Spirit," has a reference to the seven gifts of the Spirit. This beautiful prayer addresses the Holy Spirit in poetic terms: "Of comforters the best," "the soul's most welcome guest," "sweet refreshment here below," "In our labor, rest most sweet," "grateful coolness in the heat," and "solace in the midst of woe." The sequence then offers a series of petitions, including "On the faithful, who adore and confess you, evermore in your sevenfold gift descend."

In his treatment of the gifts of the Holy Spirit, Thomas Aquinas describes the gift of fortitude as a "firmness of mind in doing good and avoiding evil,"[6] particularly when it is difficult or dangerous to do so. It even strengthens Christians to face death for the sake of attaining everlasting life. Thus, martyrs for the faith are prime witnesses to the remarkable power of this gift.

Pope Francis begins his meditation on the gift of fortitude by recalling the parable of the sower and the seed.[7] The sower represents God the Father, who "abundantly sows the seed of his Word," although it "often meets with the aridity of our heart" and remains fallow. The pope says the gift of fortitude "liberates the soil of our heart," freeing it "from sluggishness, from uncertainty and from all the forces that can hinder it, so that the Lord's Word may be put into practice authentically and with joy."

Francis honors "our many brothers and sisters, past and present," who "have not hesitated to give their very lives in order to remain faithful to the Lord and his Gospel." He also honors the "everyday saints" who, strengthened by the gift of fortitude, courageously overcome obstacles and meet their daily responsibilities to earn a living, care for their families, and educate their

---

6. *Catechism of the Catholic Church*, §1806.
7. Pope Francis, General Audience, May 14, 2014, www.vatican.va.

children. These Christians, "who live in hidden holiness," are indeed a great source of inspiration, encouraging us to ask God for the gift of fortitude so that we can face our specific difficulties and personal fears steadfastly and bravely.

As we try to make fortitude the "tenor of our Christian life in the ordinary daily routine," we do well to recall the words of the apostle Paul: "I can do all things through him who strengthens me" (Phil 4:13).

Let us reflect on this striking example of Christian courage. Sister Dorothy Stang, SND, born in 1931 in Dayton, Ohio, dedicated her life to serving the rural poor in the Amazon Basin of Brazil and defending the Brazilian rainforest from depletion by loggers and wealthy landowners. Despite frequent death threats, she remained faithful to this ministry for almost four decades. On the morning of February 12, 2005, two gunmen hired by an angry landowner murdered her with multiple shots as she walked alone on a dirt road heading for a meeting.

Consider another example of Christian fortitude. A Catholic couple warmly invited a Black family into their all-white neighborhood, well aware that it would anger many of their neighbors. Such examples of unsung courage can inspire all of us to overcome our fears and live the gospel in challenging situations.

*What threats in the world today require me to rely on the Holy Spirit and the gift of fortitude?*

# KNOWLEDGE

Thomas Aquinas not only wrote subtle analyses of the seven gifts of the Holy Spirit but also composed beautiful prayers asking the Spirit for these gifts. For example:

Come, Holy Spirit, true source of light and fountain
  of wisdom.
Pour forth your brilliance upon my dense intellect,
dissipate the darkness which covers me,
that of sin and ignorance.
Grant me a penetrating mind to understand
and the lucidity to grasp things correctly and
  fundamentally.

In his *Summa Theologiae*, Aquinas recognizes the gift
of "knowledge" as one of the seven gifts that Isaiah ascribed to
the promised Messiah (see Isa 11:1–2). For Thomas, the gift of
knowledge enables us to make correct judgments about what to
believe and how we should act in accord with God's will. Following Augustine, Thomas distinguishes the gift of wisdom, which is
about divine things, from the gift of knowledge, which is about
human affairs, helping us make good judgments and follow the
"straight path of justice."

In his treatment of the gift of knowledge, Pope Francis
focuses on ways that the "beauty of nature" and the "grandeur of
the cosmos" alert us to the "greatness and love of God," arousing
in us a "profound sense of gratitude." The first chapter of Genesis
tells us that God thought everything he made "was good," especially the male and female humans, who were "very good" (Gen
1:31). "The gift of knowledge," says Francis, "sets us in profound
harmony with the Creator," allowing us "to participate in the clar-
ity of his vision and his judgment" and to recognize others as
"brothers and sisters."[8]

The pope goes on to encourage us to follow the example
of Saint Francis of Assisi, who knew how to offer joyful praise to
God through the contemplation of nature. Since creation is a

---

8. Pope Francis, General Audience, May 21, 2014, www.vatican.va.

marvelous gift from God, we must care for it and "harness it for the benefit of all, always with great respect and gratitude."

The gift of knowledge enables us to recognize that all things are potentially revelatory and to appreciate the depth dimension of the full range of human experience. This includes not only the grandeur of nature but also the richness of human relationships; not only noteworthy events but also the tedium of daily life; not only the joys of life but also the sorrows; not only sacred moments but also secular ones.

Let us envision individuals who have more fully cooperated with the Holy Spirit's gift of knowledge and expanded their perception of God at work in their lives. For example, a married woman who generally feels God's presence at Mass came to see her marital relationship as graced. An artist who sometimes experiences divine inspiration in his work came to recognize the Spirit present in the ups and downs of everyday family life. A grandmother who relied on God's help in the difficult task of raising her four children now thanks God for the deep joy her grandchildren bring her. An elderly man who was always very grateful for the gift of good health developed a greater sense of dependence on God as he contended with the diminishments of aging.

*How does the gift of knowledge help me recognize the potential for progress in our changing world?*

# PIETY

In general, Western Christian spirituality has maintained a strong Christocentric focus, with less emphasis on the role of the Holy Spirit than in Eastern Christianity. In the West, we typically pray to God the Father through Christ our Lord. Eastern Christians typically pray in the Holy Spirit, through Jesus to God the Father. Pope John Paul II urged Western Catholics to "breathe out of both lungs," meaning that we should dialogue with the Orthodox churches and learn from their distinctive spirituality, including their devotion to the Holy Spirit.

The apostle Paul reminded the Christians in Corinth that one and the same Spirit bestowed various gifts on each of them to be used to proclaim the Lordship of Christ and to serve the common good (see 1 Cor 12:1–31). The Second Vatican Council taught that the Holy Spirit remains active in the Church today, enabling believers "to have access to the Father through Christ." The Spirit "dwells in the Church and in the hearts of the faithful as in a temple," equipping them with special gifts that benefit the whole community. We should accept these gifts or "charisms," both simple and outstanding ones, with a sense of gratitude and consolation. By its emphasis on the Spirit, the council reminds us that we are all called to holiness and are all responsible for building up the Body of Christ and spreading the kingdom in the world (*Lumen Gentium* 4–12).

Saints Augustine and Aquinas emphasized the seven gifts of the Spirit, mentioned in the Book of Isaiah, including the gift of "piety" that moves us to reverence and worship God our Father and to love his daughters and sons, our sisters and brothers.

Pope Francis reminds us that our relationship with God is not a "duty or imposition" but a "friendship lived with the heart," which changes our lives, filling us with "passion and joy." Authentic piety should not be confused with a "pietism" that is unrealistic and pretends to be holy. It is, rather, a gift that enables us to be "humble of heart" and to love with "filial trust" as God's children. It makes us capable of "rejoicing with those who rejoice, weeping with those who weep, of being close to those who are lonely or in anguish, of correcting those in error, of consoling the afflicted, of welcoming and helping those in need."[9] The gift of

---

9. Pope Francis, General Audience, June 4, 2014, www.vatican.va.

piety inclines us to worship God with joy in our heart and serve our neighbor with a smile on our face.

We can see the gift of piety in parishioners who enjoy coming to Mass, who listen attentively to the scripture readings and homily, who share a warm greeting of peace, who receive communion with an open heart, who go out of their way to greet a stranger after Mass, and who try to live the gospel message during the week.

We can also detect the Holy Spirit tugging at the heart of those who struggle to pay attention to the homily, who overcome reluctance and extend the sign of peace, who ask for the gift of faith as they receive communion, who leave church with good intentions, and who try to stay patient leaving the crowded parking lot.

*How can the gift of piety help me maintain a positive, joyful attitude in a world threatened by continuing violence and personal despair?*

# FEAR OF THE LORD

The last of the seven gifts of the Holy Spirit is "fear of the Lord." For Christians uncomfortable with the word *fear*, it is helpful to note that the original Hebrew can refer to reverential respect for the awesome love God lavishes on us. Following Augustine, Thomas Aquinas distinguishes "servile fear," which is deleterious to a healthy spirituality, from "filial fear," which is a gift of the Holy Spirit enabling us to reverence God and follow the divine will. The more we love God, the more open we are to the promptings of the Holy Spirit and the less fearful we are of divine punishment, for the New Testament teaches us that "love casts out fear" (1 John 4:18).

Following Aquinas and his own pastoral instincts, Pope Francis begins his meditation on this gift of fear of the Lord by insisting that it does not mean being afraid of God, since our heavenly

Father wants our salvation and is always ready to forgive us. It does remind us of "how small we are before God" and that "our good lies in humble, respectful and trusting self-abandonment into his hands."[10] It makes us feel like children in the arms of a loving God, "enfolded and sustained" by divine warmth and protection. By accepting our own limitations, we open our minds and hearts to the Spirit, who "comforts us" and leads us to "follow the Lord with humility, docility, and obedience." This gift of the Spirit does not make us "shy and submissive" or instill an "attitude of resignation, passivity or regret," but stirs within us the "wonder and joy" of being a child of God and prompts us to act with "courage and strength."[11]

Francis also views the gift of reverential fear as "an alarm against the obstinacy of sin"—for example, exploiting others and living only for money, vanity, power, or pride, none of which we can take with us to the "other side." Finally, Pope Francis adds a prayer that all of us will "welcome the gift of fear of the Lord," which prompts us both to trust our merciful Father and to respect our just judge.

Consider, for example, a Catholic grandmother, who lived in servile fear of God for much of her life, worried about mortal sins and the fires of hell. Later in life, influenced by her daughter with a degree in theology, she gradually came to see God more as a loving Father, who speaks to us through Christ, our friend, and who calls us to make a generous response to the promptings of the Holy Spirit.

An ambitious, rising corporate executive, blessed with a loving wife, ignored his Catholic training and for years lived a self-centered life, while taking advantage of his wife's compassionate, forgiving nature. Recognizing the unhealthy state of their marriage, she used all her leverage to get him into marriage counseling

---

10. Pope Francis, General Audience, June 11, 2014, www.vatican.va.

11. Pope Francis, General Audience, June 11, 2014, www.vatican.va.

with a priest, who told him straight out that he better change his selfish lifestyle because one day the just Judge would demand an accounting. This pointed admonition struck home, and the husband made a commitment to start a long and arduous process of reform, guided by the Holy Spirit and the gift of fear of the Lord.

*How can reverential fear of the Lord help me meet my responsibilities in a society filled with new challenges?*

# 5

## The Beatitudes

According to the *Catechism*, the Beatitudes represent the heart of Jesus's preaching. "They take up the promises made to the chosen people since Abraham and fulfill the promises by ordering them no longer to the possession of a territory, but to the Kingdom of heaven" (§1717).

When Jesus saw the crowds, he went up the mountain; and after he sat down, his disciples came to him. Then he began to speak, and taught them, saying:

"Blessed are the poor in spirit, for theirs is the kingdom of heaven.
"Blessed are those who mourn, for they will be comforted.
"Blessed are the meek, for they will inherit the earth.
"Blessed are those who hunger and thirst for righteousness, for they will be filled.
"Blessed are the merciful, for they will receive mercy.

"Blessed are the pure in heart, for they will see God.
"Blessed are the peacemakers, for they will be called
children of God.
"Blessed are those who are persecuted for
righteousness' sake, for theirs is the kingdom of
heaven.
"Blessed are you when people revile you and
persecute you and utter all kinds of evil against you
falsely on my account. Rejoice and be glad, for
your reward is great in heaven." (Matt 5:1–12)

Furthermore, "the Beatitudes depict the countenance of
Jesus Christ and portray his charity. They express the vocation of
the faithful associated with the glory of his Passion and Resurrection; they shed light on the actions and attitudes characteristic of
the Christian life; they are the paradoxical promises that sustain
hope in the midst of tribulations; they proclaim the blessings and
rewards already secured, however dimly, for Christ's disciples;
they have begun in the lives of the Virgin Mary and all the saints"
(§1717).

# BLESSED ARE THE POOR IN SPIRIT

This is the first of eight Beatitudes at the beginning of the
Sermon on the Mount (Matthew 5 – 7), written around fifty years
after the death of Jesus. According to scholars, Matthew, who was
not an eyewitness to the life of Jesus, drew on two sources for his
material: the Gospel of Mark and a hypothetical collection of
sayings of Jesus, known as the Q document. We do not have the
actual document, but scholars can reconstruct part of it by iden-
tifying passages that are similar in Matthew and Luke but not in
Mark. The fact that Matthew and Luke, written independently

in the 80s, share some identical passages indicates that they have a common written source. The ways they differ in their use of Q suggests something of their own theological perspective. Hypothetical Q includes crucial passages not in Mark and John, such as the Lord's Prayer and the Beatitudes.

While Matthew has eight Beatitudes, Luke, in a parallel passage, has only four, and his first one simply states, "Blessed are the poor," without the phrase "in spirit." Many scholars think Luke is more faithful to Q and that Matthew has softened and spiritualized that original document. In his provocative book *Spirituality of the Beatitudes* (2005), Michael Crosby argues that Matthew made a wise pastoral move by adding "in spirit" because it made the first beatitude more relevant for the well-to-do members of his community and, by extension, affluent Christians today. Matthew helps us see poverty in perspective. Material poverty is not in itself a good thing; it is ungodly, not what God wants for human beings. Those who are well off should not romanticize the life of the poor as being uncluttered or carefree. Nor should we see poverty as a difficult way of life that by God's plan leads to the abundant life of heaven. In Matthew, Jesus does not praise the poor, nor does he advocate poverty as an end. He does, however, advocate care for the poor and promises salvation to those who try to help them.

For Matthew, the poor in spirit are those who recognize their total dependence on God, who abandon themselves to God's loving care, and who try to do God's will in all things. They overcome the Satanic temptation to be like God and control their own lives. Instead, they empty themselves, as did Jesus, and submit themselves to God's rule, his kingdom of love, justice, and peace.

The poor in spirit reorder their personal and social lives. Abandoning false securities, they commit themselves to assist those suffering from the burdens of material poverty. They use nonviolent strategies to challenge societal structures that imprison people in miserable conditions. They try to empower the poor to take hold of their own lives so that they can share in God's kingdom of justice and peace.

In response to this analysis of the first beatitude, an affluent man, who for years has consistently tuned out Catholic Social Teaching on the poor because it made him feel guilty, could come to see that the Church does not condemn the wealthy but calls them to find generous and wise ways to use their blessings to help the less fortunate. A middle-class couple, who generally take their comfortable lifestyle for granted, could decide to volunteer at a soup kitchen once a week as a way of both reminding themselves of God's many blessings and helping the needy.

*How can Matthew's first beatitude help me deal with the inequalities in our world today?*

# BLESSED ARE THOSE WHO MOURN

Our English word *blessed* translates the original Greek *makarios*, which suggests a state of happiness flowing from being in right relationships with God and the community. The Hebrew scriptures contain many beatitudes based on trusting God. For example, "Happy are those who make the LORD their trust" (Ps 40:4), and "Happy are those whose help is the God of Jacob, whose hope is in the LORD their God" (Ps 146:5). There are also references that set the stage for the New Testament Beatitudes. In the Book of Isaiah, for instance, the Suffering Servant declares that the Spirit of the Lord is upon him to preach good news to the poor and "to comfort all who mourn" (Isa 61:2).

The New Testament has more than forty beatitudes, including these eight in Matthew, that generally stress the happiness of participating in God's kingdom. The New Testament scholar Raymond Brown tells us that Matthew's Beatitudes do not refer to blessings received from God for proper behavior. Specifically, the second beatitude does not promise comfort for properly mourning some specific suffering. The Beatitudes do, however, recognize an existing state of happiness and blessing that accompanies living the truth and values taught by Jesus and honored by the Christian community—a partial state of bliss to be totally fulfilled in the eternal life of heaven. Indeed, blessed, happy, and honored are those who follow the example of Jesus and treat the suffering with compassion, who help form communities sensitive to suffering members, and who are committed to reducing the pool of suffering in the world.

In a talk on the second beatitude, Pope Francis insisted that authentic mourning flows from personal suffering, from experiencing afflictions, and from the "gift of tears" that enables us to bond with those who suffer, allowing them to "enter our heart." This beatitude challenges those who have "a heart of stone and have forgotten how to cry."[1] The inability to mourn the suffering of others forces us into isolation and inhibits authentic relationships. For some, the loss of a loved one is so intense, so painful, that they cannot face it, cannot enter a healthy grieving process, and cannot mourn properly. The second beatitude encourages all of us to learn from the example of Jesus, who wept at the death of his friend Lazarus, to find needed support from compassionate Church members, and to pray for greater trust in God, who sends us the Holy Spirit, the Comforter.

Consider, for example, a widow who has worked her way through a difficult grieving process after the sudden death of her sixty-year-old husband and is now living a satisfying life, continuing her career as a teacher, serving on the parish liturgy committee, and enjoying her children and grandchildren. Or a devoted husband, who has always cared for his wife, visits and feeds her

---

1. Pope Francis, General Audience, February 12, 2020, www.vatican.va.

most days now that she is in a memory care center and no longer recognizes him. We can also consider a social activist, who cannot stand to watch violence on television, stays active in Pax Christi, and periodically joins protests against racial injustice. And finally, the father, who showed little understanding of his daughter's bulimia struggle but decided to learn more about it and became a welcomed, compassionate presence to her striving to develop healthy eating patterns.

*How can I become a more compassionate person in a world filled with suffering?*

# BLESSED ARE THE MEEK

Matthew's third beatitude is a direct reference to verse 22 of Psalm 37, which compares the fate of the just and the wicked: "For those blessed by the LORD shall inherit the land, but those cursed by him shall be cut off." The Psalmist is referring to Israel taking possession of the promised land, while Matthew is talking about inheriting the kingdom, which is received as a gift but not possessed or controlled. Matthew's original Greek, translated as "meek," can also mean gentle, humble, and nonviolent. Later in the Gospel, Jesus offers these comforting words to those heavily burdened: "Take my yoke upon you, and learn from me; for I am gentle and humble in heart, and you will find rest for your souls" (Matt 11:29).

Historically, the Christian ideal of meekness has been criticized for encouraging believers to be weak, cowardly, accommodating, and afraid to face the harsh realities of life. For example, the nineteenth-century philosopher Friedrich Nietzsche criticized meekness as a false value part of a "slave morality" that keeps believers from creating their own values and becoming authentic, powerful individuals.[2] Christian apologists have responded to this form of criticism. Augustine, for example, argued that the meek wisely avoid fighting over earthly goods and conserve their energy to overcome evil with good. Eastern Doctor of the Church John Chrysostom claimed that "nothing is more powerful than meekness" because it enables us to control our anger and to reconcile with others.

In a contemporary context, Pope Francis also stresses the inherent power of Christian meekness that enables us to manage stressful situations when we are attacked, offended, and threatened. The pope reminds us that the apostle Paul highlighted "the meekness and gentleness of Christ," whom we recognize as the most powerful force for human liberation and fulfillment in all history. As Christians, we are called to imitate the meekness of Jesus by protecting and extending God's reign in the world, our inherited home. The meek can promote kingdom values because they are "merciful, fraternal people with hope."[3] Francis emphasizes the role of meekness in controlling our anger, which can be so destructive and can ruin our relationships with our brothers and sisters. The pope advises us to calm down, think things over, and retrace our steps, conscious that "anger separates" but "meekness brings people together" and enables us to rebuild relationships. In the inherited land of God's kingdom, meekness is seen not as weakness but as power, not as servile but as liberating, not as dehumanizing but as fulfilling.

Individuals can demonstrate the power of meekness in various ways. Consider, for example, a man who has been estranged from his sister for years. He could offer to treat her to dinner and talk things over. Or a wife, who has been overly subservient to her husband out of a questionable understanding of Christian

---

2. See "Nietzsche's Ethics," *Internet Encyclopedia of Philosophy*, https://iep.utm.edu/nietzsches-ethics/.

3. Pope Francis, General Audience, February 19, 2020, www.vatican.va.

meekness, could take the first step forward by talking to her husband about her new perception of their relationship. There is the example of a collegian, who still has a childish dependency on his mother and father. He could begin a process of establishing a more adult relationship with his parents. Finally, there is the example of a corporate executive who periodically blows up at her coworkers. She could spend a few minutes each day on the way to work asking Christ to help her practice meekness and control her anger.

*How can I practice the virtue of meekness in a culture that celebrates raw power?*

# BLESSED ARE THOSE WHO HUNGER AND THIRST FOR RIGHTEOUSNESS

The words "hunger and thirst" refer to the deepest longings of the human heart. The Greek philosopher Aristotle taught that all human beings seek "happiness" as their goal. The Psalmist identified God as the goal of our most profound longings. "My soul thirsts for God, for the living God" (Ps 42:2) and "O God, you are my God, I seek you, my soul thirsts for you" (Ps 63:1). In his commentary on the fourth beatitude, Augustine references the conversation between Jesus and the Samaritan woman at the well, where Jesus tells her, "Everyone who drinks of this water will be thirsty again, but those who drink of the water that I will give them will never be thirsty. The water that I will give will become in them a spring of water gushing up to eternal life" (John 4:13–14). Augustine reminds us that we have a spiritual thirst greater than any bodily thirst and that it can be fulfilled only by the gift of eternal life in union with God. In his *Confessions*, Augustine famously prayed, "You have made us for yourself, O Lord, and our heart is restless until it rests in you." Our innate hunger and thirst create an inner anxiety, a restlessness that can be totally satisfied only in heaven, even though we can experience fulfilling moments on this earth.

In the Old Testament, the Hebrew word translated as "righteousness" is frequently used in the context of God's gracious covenant relationship with Israel. Yahweh, the Lord God, is himself righteous, always faithful to his promise to save his people and make them a great nation. In turn, the Israelites are called to live righteously by doing God's will and keeping God's commandments.

In the New Testament, John the Baptist, who called Israel to repentance, agreed to baptize Jesus "to fulfill all righteousness" (Matt 3:15). Jesus himself was the righteous one who proclaimed the kingdom of justice and peace. In Matthew, when Jesus tells his disciples to hunger and thirst for righteousness, he is calling us to commit ourselves to doing God's will, to spreading his kingdom, and to fulfilling the divine plan to save all people. To live this commitment in accord with the highest ideals of the Christian community is to know a measure of fulfillment that will be complete only in eternal life with God.

Appropriating the deep truth represented by this beatitude could prompt individual conversions. A lawyer passionate about making money and gaining fame, for example, could see the light and become committed to the great cause of doing justice. A lukewarm Catholic could get serious about fulfilling Christ's command to love God and neighbor. A young man obsessed with pleasing his father could decide to follow God's call to be his own best person. And a citizen unreasonably loyal to her political party could reorder her priorities to put God, faith, family, and nation before any party.

*How can I live the fourth beatitude more faithfully on my spiritual journey?*

# BLESSED ARE THE MERCIFUL

The Beatitudes—the heart of Christ's message—indicate specific ways he fulfilled God's promises to the chosen people. For example, the fifth beatitude directs our attention to Jesus, who fulfills God's pledge of unconditional mercy to the Israelites by extending mercy to many individuals he encountered during his public ministry.

When the scribes and Pharisees, for example, try to trap Jesus by asking if the woman caught in adultery should be stoned, Jesus famously declares, "Let anyone among you who is without sin be the first to throw a stone at her," and then, when alone with the woman, he assures her that he does not condemn her and admonishes her not to sin anymore (see John 8:1–11). Matthew tells the story of a man full of leprosy who asks Jesus to make him clean. Jesus, reaching out to touch him, declares, "Be made clean!" and he is instantly cured (Matt 8:1–4). In Luke's Gospel, Jesus encounters a widow burying her only son and, feeling a deep visceral sense of compassion, tells her not to cry and raises her son to life, affording her not only joy and comfort but also security and protection in that patriarchal culture (see Luke 7:11–17).

In Mark, when Jesus sees a vast crowd, he has "compassion for them, because they were like sheep without a shepherd" and begins to "teach them many things." When it gets late, Jesus once again has mercy on the crowd by feeding them all with five loaves and two fish (Mark 6:34–44). Jesus maintains his ministry of mercy right to the end of his life when he assures the repentant thief: "Truly I tell you, today you will be with me in Paradise" (Luke 23:39–43). As these examples indicate, Jesus Christ himself is divine mercy incarnate—the human face of God's forgiving love and our example of compassionate care for those in need.

The fifth beatitude also suggests the essential connection between mercy received and mercy shared. In the Lord's Prayer, we dare to ask God to "forgive us our trespasses as we forgive those who trespass against us." Recognizing the many ways God has had mercy on us and forgiven our sins should move us to extend this great blessing to others. Mercy should be contagious, spreading abundantly through the Christian community. The Church should be a credible sign and effective instrument of the mercy Christ extended to all people.

We are blessed with many vibrant parishes that do indeed reflect Christ's mercy in significant ways: facilitating access to the physically disabled; welcoming individuals who may feel alienated, such as members of the LGBTQ community; providing a meal after funeral Masses for grieving parishioners; offering adult education for those seeking to understand their faith; sponsoring support groups for the divorced, bereaved, and others facing a common challenge; and preaching homilies that stress God's mercy and forgiveness.

*How can I help my parish be a better sign of Christ's divine mercy?*

# BLESSED ARE THE PURE IN HEART

There is general agreement that the word *heart* is a fundamental "primordial" symbol in the Bible, representing the primary bodily focus of emotional reactions and intellectual knowledge. In the New Testament, Christ enlightens the eyes of our hearts and, along with the Father, sends the Holy Spirit to dwell in our hearts. Some commentators, such as Augustine and Thomas Merton, stress the need for a calm spirit and a tranquil mind in order to see the God who dwells within us. Other scholars emphasize that having a pure heart means being "single-minded" in living our Christian faith. A prime example of this approach is the nineteenth-century Danish philosopher Søren Kierkegaard

(1813–1855), who wrote an essay, "Purity of Heart Is to Will One Thing," which he intended to function like a sermon that would both build us up and challenge us.

In general, Kierkegaard, a critic of the "lenient Christianity" practiced by the Danish Lutheran Church, encouraged cultural Christians to become authentic Christians, individuals dedicated to doing the "One Thing," variously described as pursuing the Good, appreciating the Eternal, doing God's will, and spreading God's kingdom. More specifically, his essay suggests ways of moving toward a greater purity of heart and a more single-minded practice of the Christian faith that can be expressed in the following series of contemporary admonitions and suggested actions:

- Maintain an abiding sense of the "Eternal" in the temporal unfolding of your daily lives, recognizing the depth dimension of the full range of your experience. Action: share a prayer of gratitude before the family dinner, recalling God's many blessings throughout the day.

- Do what is truly good and avoid making an idol out of any finite reality, such as fame, wealth, pleasure, and ambition. Action: do an honest self-examination of your priorities, looking for imbalances; write down how many hours you spend each day on work, family, personal concerns, and serving the community.

- Recognize your sinfulness, including sins of omission; show remorse; repent; and confess your sins. Action: celebrate the sacrament of penance or apologize to someone you hurt or offended.

- Do not expect to become single-minded in one big unmistakable encounter with God sometime in the future; strive for purity of heart in the here

and now of the ordinary situations of everyday life.
Action: make a conscious effort to see your work
as a catalyst for self-actualization and a means of
spreading God's reign in the world.

- Accept the inevitable sufferings of life; strive to
reduce suffering and trust that God is with you
amid suffering. Action: complain less about your
problems or help a neighbor in need.

- Be yourself, follow your own unique path to holiness, do not follow the crowd, and avoid group-
think. Action: write a personal Christian creed,
noting beliefs that are most relevant; learn how to
disagree amiably with friends and relatives.

- Befriend death as an opportunity to make definitive and total your choice of God as your true goal.
Action: try to gracefully accept diminishments of
life as preparation for your death.

*How can I become more single-minded in living my faith in a
culture that celebrates keeping our options open?*

# BLESSED ARE THE PEACEMAKERS

Matthew's seventh beatitude reflects the life and teachings
of Jesus, who is the supreme peacemaker. Jesus teaches us the
power of nonviolent responses to the dark forces that assail us.
At his arrest by armed men, Jesus responded to Peter's violent
resistance, "Put your sword back into its place; for all who take
the sword will perish by the sword" (Matt 26:52). Christ, the
Prince of Peace, also taught us to "turn the other cheek" and not
to meet force with force (see Matt 5:38–42). In his farewell talk to

his disciples, Jesus said, "Peace I leave with you; my peace I give to you. I do not give to you as the world gives" (John 14:27).

Christ is not calling us to be passive in the face of evil and suffering or to ignore the violent conflicts around our world. Nor does Christ's peace simply sanction the fragile peace today between nations with immense stockpiles of nuclear weapons. As Catholic Social Teaching now makes clear, genuine Christian peace is based on justice. In the often-repeated words of Pope Paul VI: "If you want peace, work for justice." Concretely, justice involves respecting the dignity of every person, guaranteeing the rights of minorities, lifting more people out of poverty, overcoming prejudice, empowering those who are marginalized, and assisting developing countries. Systemic injustice sets the stage for violence; progress toward greater justice prepares the way for true peace.

This beatitude functions as a personal call to action. Christ offers us the gift of his peace, but we must cooperate with God's grace to make it a reality. As baptized Christians, our vocation is to spread God's reign of justice and peace in the world. The 1971 Synod of Bishops taught that "Action on behalf of justice" is a "constitutive dimension of the preaching of the Gospel." Likewise, we can say that peacemaking is an essential dimension of living an authentic Christian life. We all have a moral obligation to promote peace in our own circle of influence.

Let us imagine individual Christians meeting this responsibility. Consider a husband in a rocky marriage who consistently apologizes after a fight and looks for ways to restore a measure of peace. Ponder a small-business owner who brings together two of her quarrelling employees to talk out their problems and treat each other civilly on the job. We think of a man who is estranged from a former friend in the neighborhood but achieved a peaceful reconciliation by inviting him to his house to watch a Notre Dame football game and enjoy a few beers together. Or consider a city council member who overcame partisan rancor and formed a civil working relationship with a council colleague. And finally, think of the parishioner who joined Pax Christi to be part of a group advocating for nonviolent, peaceful solutions to national and international conflicts.

*How can I meet my Christian responsibility to be a peace-maker in a world threatened by strife and violence?*

# BLESSED ARE THOSE WHO ARE PERSECUTED

New Testament scholars tell us that the next verse is not a separate ninth beatitude but an effort to make this eighth beatitude more personal by changing the pronoun from "they" to "you": "Blessed are you when people revile you and persecute you and utter all kinds of evil against you falsely on my account. Rejoice and be glad, for your reward is great in heaven, for in the same way they persecuted the prophets who were before you" (Matt 5:11–12). Matthew saw Jesus as the definitive prophet, who was persecuted and executed by the authorities threatened by his righteous proclamations of God's reign. The evangelist may also have had in mind earlier conflicts between the Jewish establishment and the growing Christian community they considered heretical. Christian history is filled with stories of martyrs, ranging from Saint Peter in the first century to Archbishop Óscar Romero in the twentieth. The international organization Open Doors reports that, in a recent one-year period, more than 4,700 Christians were martyred worldwide and 4,200 were detained or imprisoned. Persecutions take place in over fifty countries, including North Korea, Nigeria, and China. In the United States, the First Amendment has enabled Christianity to flourish without fear of persecution. Furthermore, Christian faith is in accord with important aspects of American life, for example, the idealism of the Declaration of Independence as well as some cultural values, such as hard work and personal freedom.

Christian faith, however, is also in tension with other current trends in the United States—for example, clearly anti-gospel positions, such as sexism, racism, homophobia, and xenophobia. Christians have a responsibility to oppose these destructive ideologies even at personal cost. We know people who have done that. A white married couple with two children went ahead with adopting a young Black boy, even though their parents on both sides objected and vowed not to accept the boy as their grandchild. A woman challenged the sexist promotion policies of her company, even though it created a stressful adversarial relationship with her boss. A man befriended a gay colleague at work, even though straight coworkers continued to ridicule him for doing so. And a family in Texas took in a refugee couple from Honduras, even though their neighbors objected.

Politically, many Catholics in the United States do not feel totally comfortable in either party. Some pro-life Democrats who accept the Catholic position on abortion are at odds with their party's support for abortion rights and its opposition to the Hyde Amendment prohibiting the use of federal funds for abortion. Some Republicans who accept the position of Pope Francis on climate change feel out of step with their party's support for fossil fuel industries.

Catholic Social Teaching (CST) criticizes our modern neoliberal economic system for not doing more to serve the common good and the needs of the poor. Pope Francis, for example, is critical of "trickle down" theories claiming that economic growth generated by the free market will inevitably produce greater justice and inclusion. Catholics who adhere to CST can find themselves at odds with popular opinion. For example, a religion teacher in a Catholic high school, who taught a class on CST to seniors that included common criticisms of economic liberalism, received significant harsh criticism from parents accusing him of advocating Marxist socialism.

*Do I ever feel tension between my Catholic faith and my life as an American citizen?*

# 6

# Celebrations

The *Catechism* teaches that "the Church celebrates in the liturgy above all the Paschal mystery by which Christ accomplished the work of our salvation. The word *liturgy* comes from a Greek term meaning 'public work or work done on behalf of the people.'" Consequently, "all the worshipers are expected to participate actively in each liturgy, for this is holy 'work,' not entertainment or a spectator event....It therefore requires the participation of the People of God in the work of God."[1] Furthermore, "through the liturgical celebrations of the Church, we participate in the Paschal Mystery of Christ, that is, his passing through death from this life into eternal glory, just as God enabled the people of ancient Israel to pass from slavery to freedom through the events narrated in the Book of Exodus (see Exod 11—13). The liturgies of the Church also help to teach us about Jesus Christ and the meaning of the mysteries we are celebrating....It is the Holy Spirit, the source of the Church's life, who draws us together through liturgical actions, the chief of which are the Sacraments."[2]

---

1. *Catechism of the Catholic Church*, §§1066–67.
2. *United States Catholic Catechism for Adults*, 195.

# LITURGICAL CELEBRATIONS

## Lent

### *Ash Wednesday*

Ash Wednesday is the traditional beginning of Lent, the penitential season that prepares us for a celebration of Easter. Lent is a great season for cooperating with God's grace by forming a plan for spiritual growth. It might be helpful to choose a Lenten penance or spiritual exercise that will help us grow spiritually, to become a better person and a more dedicated Christian by the time we celebrate the resurrection on Easter. Based on the Gospel reading for Ash Wednesday (Matt 6:1–6, 16–18), we traditionally refer to three types of Lenten practices: almsgiving, prayer, and fasting.

Let us imagine ways of making almsgiving, which includes all types of charitable deeds, a more effective instrument of continued spiritual growth. Parishioners who give generously to the Catholic Campaign for Human Development could make use of the campaign's educational materials to learn more about the root causes of poverty in our affluent country. Parishioners who donate food bags for the hungry could volunteer to serve meals at a food distribution center. A financially secure family could adopt a family in need and offer needed assistance throughout the year.

Prayer, both liturgical and private, is a gift of God that requires our cooperation. Let us consider ways we can deepen our prayer life during the Lenten season and beyond. Liturgically, those who attend Mass sporadically could use Lent to get into the habit of going regularly. Those who usually go on Sundays could improve their participation in various ways: spending time before Mass reflecting on the scripture readings; offering a specific personal struggle, such as overcoming an addiction or bad habit, to God at the offertory; choosing one specific lesson from the Liturgy of the Word to practice during the week, such as being more charitable to friends and family members.

Lent also offers an opportunity to improve our private prayer life by setting time aside each day for prayer, spending more time silently listening to God, saying more prayers of praise and thanksgiving along with petitions, or saying brief prayers throughout the day bringing God's abiding presence to mind.

Fasting, which includes all forms of voluntary renunciation, is a traditional Lenten practice. Instead of giving up what we most crave, like desserts or cigarettes or alcohol, we could fast from something as part of a plan to develop better enduring habits: for instance, giving up a favorite food as part of a plan to develop a healthier diet; limiting time watching television to spend more time in prayer and meditation; spending less money shopping in order to increase charitable giving; limiting time on social media in order to develop better face-to-face communication skills; avoiding gossip in order to become a more charitable person; and fasting from harsh political rhetoric as a way of becoming a better citizen.

*What specific Lenten practice is most likely to help me become a more faithful Christian on my spiritual journey?*

## The Triduum

The Church year reaches its high point in the liturgical celebration of Holy Thursday, Good Friday, and Easter, often referred to by the Latin phrase *Triduum* [Tri-doo-oom] or Sacred Three Days. The forty-day Lenten penitential season prepares us for the *Triduum*, and the fifty-day Easter season provides time for reflection on its meaning and application for our spiritual journey. During the pandemic, many Catholics who usually participate in the *Triduum* were not able to do so. In many parishes, important parts of the liturgy were not celebrated: the washing of the feet on Holy Thursday, the veneration of the cross on Good Friday, and the blessing of the fire at the Easter Vigil. For those who could not participate fully in the church services, it was possible to celebrate a *Triduum* of the world, taking time during each of the three days to reflect on ways we have experienced the meaning of the feasts in our everyday lives.

On Holy Thursday, we traditionally celebrate the Mass of the Lord's Supper, which, along with Good Friday and Easter, constitute the Paschal Triduum, the most important liturgical celebrations of the year. The epistle for this day (1 Cor 11:23–26) is the oldest written account of the Last Supper, composed about two decades after the event, and recalls the institution of the eucharistic meal by Christ and his repeated command: "Do this in remembrance of me."

The Gospel (John 13:1–15) recounts the story of how Jesus gathered his disciples for a final meal before his pending death. During the meal, he washed the feet of his disciples, including the reluctant Peter. After this symbolic gesture, Jesus pointedly told his disciples, "So if I, your Lord and Teacher, have washed your feet, you also ought to wash one another's feet" (v. 14). Jesus, who stated clearly that he came not to be served but to serve others, maintained that fundamental attitude throughout his life, right up to his last days, symbolically washing feet and freely accepting death on the cross as an unavoidable byproduct of his life of service to the cause of God and the whole human family.

When we remember Christ at Mass, we do well to recall his life of service and his command to follow his example. By celebrating the eucharistic liturgy, we express our love of God and our commitment to love our neighbor. Receiving Communion unites us to Christ and nourishes us for the demanding task of serving those we meet each day. The liturgy is communal public worship, which by its very nature calls us to serve the common good and the needs of others, including family, friends, strangers, and even our enemies. The Eucharist recalls both the comforting memory of Jesus, who teaches us to trust God's merciful love, and the challenging and sometimes dangerous memory of Christ, who calls us to join the fight against hatred and oppression and work for justice and peace.

During the pandemic, which precluded participation in the public celebration of the Holy Thursday liturgy, faithful Christians found various ways to practice the meaning of the feast: calling or writing those in nursing homes who could not have visitors, shopping for the homebound, providing financial assistance to relatives who lost their jobs, expressing gratitude and encouragement to health-care workers who were risking their lives, and praying for the victims of the virus and their families.

The Good Friday liturgical service proclaims the passion account from the Gospel according to John, which portrays Jesus attending to his disciples and his own mother during his passion (see John 18:1 — 19:42). According to John, Jesus dies freely, nobly, and courageously. A Good Friday liturgy of the world celebrates the ways God strengthened individuals to carry the crosses imposed by the pandemic: parents already struggling to raise their children, who graciously took on the added responsibility of assisting their elderly homebound parents; essential workers, who did their jobs even at the risk of their own lives; people who put up with the inconveniences of isolation without complaint; health-care providers, who worked extra hours caring for the large numbers of the sick. A Good Friday liturgy of the world prompts prayers of gratitude for the good example of persons who carried their COVID-19 crosses gracefully and generously.

The liturgical celebration of Easter proclaims Christ's victory over all the dark forces represented by death. The crucified Lord has been raised to a new glorified life. Through our baptism, we share in the victorious risen life of Christ. An Easter liturgy of the world celebrates many graced victories of life over death during the pandemic; those who completely recovered after suffering severe COVID-19 symptoms; those who continued to function daily despite periods of depression; those who overcame unreasonable fears and got vaccinated; those who continued to meet their daily responsibilities despite deeply grieving the loss of a loved one. An Easter liturgy of the world prompts prayers of gratitude for the life-giving power of God's grace.

*How can we best serve others in this post-pandemic era?*

# Easter

Easter celebrates the key dogma of the resurrection and is the most important celebration of the Church year. For Christians, Easter has an inherent power to deepen and expand our hope in God's promise to save us and our world. The Easter Vigil is filled with hopeful symbolism: the blessing of the fire, the procession with the paschal candle, and the singing of the triumphant Easter Proclamation. Regular Mass participants often find their hope renewed by the Easter liturgy with its festive tone, joyful music, inspiring Liturgy of the Word, and nourishing reception of the risen Lord. Catholics who go to Mass only on Christmas and Easter may be keeping alive a connection with a tradition that fostered the hope that still sustains them.

During the pandemic, many Christians were unable to participate in the Easter liturgy. Faithful believers, however, found various ways of maintaining and exercising Easter hope: watching Easter services online with as much personal engagement as possible; exercising the fundamental trust that holds families together by being extra kind to those in close proximity; recalling times when we made it through difficult situations; dealing with isolation and extra time creatively, such as engaging in deeper conversations, enjoying more leisurely family meals, reading a good book, organizing their home, and making masks; admitting any negative emotional reactions to the limitations imposed on us with hope of managing them effectively; avoiding excessive concentration on negative and depressing news, while paying more attention to the uplifting stories of heroic sacrifice and charitable deeds; maintaining concern for those suffering most, the seriously ill, the poor, the vulnerable, the individuals dying alone, and those grieving the loss of loved ones without even the comfort of a funeral service; helping someone in need; using the time to develop a deeper prayer life; envisioning a post-pandemic transformed world that is more compassionate, just, cooperative, and peaceful; and reflecting on the example of Christ, who patiently endured suffering, courageously remained faithful to his mission, and, on the cross, trustingly commended his spirit to his heavenly Father.

A post-pandemic spirituality must be grateful for the opportunity to return to liturgical services in our churches. It also must recognize the importance of living the Easter message by sanctifying everyday life, finding God in ordinary activities, using the challenges of life to grow spiritually, praising God by meeting our daily responsibilities and working for justice, and uniting our joys and sorrows with the crucified and risen Christ.

*How can we proclaim Easter hope in the contemporary world struggling with discouragement and despair?*

# Advent

## *Developing the Virtue of Patience*

The Advent season, when we await the coming of Christ, can try our patience as we deal with various delays—long lines in stores, slow deliveries, and hard-to-find presents. Advent presents a challenge to exercise the virtue of patience, which enables us to tolerate annoying things, like waiting, without getting overly upset or losing our focus on doing good.

At a spiritual level, we can begin by being more patient with God, who allows the evolving world to develop at its own pace, who follows a divine timetable not ours, and who exercises infinite patience in forgiving our sins and calling us to become our better selves. Becoming more patient with God provides a solid basis for being more patient with others and with ourselves.

As Christians, we can learn from the example of Jesus, who, remarkably, waited patiently for over thirty years before beginning his long-awaited public ministry; who refused Satan's temptation to make an instant impression by jumping off the pinnacle of the temple; who accepted his impending death, even though his mission was not yet completed; and who, though at times frustrated with his obtuse disciples, remained fundamentally patient with them, even after they abandoned him. Reflection on Christ encourages us to respect our own Spirit-driven rhythms of life and reminds us that it is possible to exercise patience despite frustrations.

We can also learn patience from the good example of others. The mother, for example, who realized she was much more prone to impatience with her children when overly fatigued, became more patient after adopting a regular exercise program, which generated more restful sleep and a calmer spirit; the salesperson, who knew he was more patient with customers than his wife, treated her more kindly when, on his way home from work, he recalled his good fortune in having such an understanding and caring wife; the father, who admitted that his quick temper caused him to say hurtful things to his children, dealt with them more respectfully when he took a few deep breaths and said a quick prayer before disciplining them; and the lifelong Catholic, who confessed impatience as his major sin, which harmed all his relationships, made improvements by regularly repeating this prayer assigned for his penance:

Gracious God, I thank you for being patient with me as I deal with the vicissitudes of daily life. Help me to be patient with my Church, which energizes and guides me but often disappoints me; my loved ones, who gladden my heart but now and then try my patience; my friends, who brighten my life but sometimes test my tolerance; and my colleagues, who help make work meaningful but periodically rub me the wrong way. I offer this prayer through Our Lord Jesus Christ, my primary guide for cultivating the virtue of patience. Amen.

*How can I become a more patient person in our fast-paced world?*

## Cultivating the Virtue of Hope

For Western Christianity, Advent is the four-week liturgical season that prepares for Christmas. Since the time of Saint Bernard of Clairvaux (d. 1153), Advent has been seen as celebrating the threefold coming of Christ, his past birth in Bethlehem, his present coming in grace, and his future coming at the end time, when he will complete his mission to save all people.

Advent has traditionally been associated with the virtue of hope. We can read the whole Bible as a story of hope based on God's absolute fidelity to the divine promises made to great leaders, especially Abraham, Moses, and David, interpreted by major prophets, such as Isaiah and Jeremiah, and fulfilled in Jesus Christ. To think of the Bible as a story of promise and fulfillment engenders hope, which highlights desire, expectation, and anticipation.

For Christians, our deepest hopes are fulfilled in Christ, who obediently accepted death on the cross and was, in fulfillment of the promise, raised to a glorious new life by his Father. The resurrection assures us that God is trustworthy and serves as a guarantee that his will to save all people will one day be accomplished.

This hope of the final victory of good over evil alerts us to signs of hope in our own lives that, in turn, strengthen our hope in the ultimate triumph of God's grace over all the dark forces that assail us.

This is indeed Advent good news for all of us tempted to discouragement in the face of persistent evil, such as global warming, international terrorism, national racism, church scandals, troubled relationships, and personal demons. Advent hope encourages us to continue to work steadfastly for good, a healthy planet, peace and justice, church reform, loving relationships, and personal integrity. We can imagine, for example, individuals making Advent fruitful by doing a better job of recycling; participating in a peace organization, such as Pax Christi; befriending a person of a different race; getting an estranged spouse to see a counselor or attending a Marriage Encounter weekend; and participating in a twelve-step program to overcome an addiction. Advent, a season rich with spiritual resources, invites all of us to turn it into an instrument and sign of hope.

*How can we make Advent a genuine sign of hope in a society continuing to struggle with persistent problems?*

# Solemnity of Mary, the Holy Mother of God

On January 1, the day many people make resolutions for the coming year, the Catholic Church liturgically celebrates the Solemnity of Mary, the Holy Mother of God. Luke's Gospel records the story of the shepherds coming to see Mary and Joseph and revealing the angelic message that the baby lying in the manger was indeed the promised Messiah (see Luke 2:10). Luke then tells us, "Mary treasured all these words and pondered them in her heart," suggesting her ongoing prayerful efforts to understand the deeper significance of her son's birth (Luke 2:19). Mary's good example could prompt a New Year's resolution to spend more time in quiet reflection and more prayer in listening to the Spirit.

Starting in 1967, the Church has also celebrated the World Day of Peace on January 1. Each year, the pope uses the occasion to address a message of peace to the global community. In 2017, Pope Francis called on Christians to embrace the example and teaching on nonviolence of Jesus, who "walked that path all the way to the cross" and "became our peace."[3] For Francis, nonviolence does not mean passivity or surrendering to evil, but rather actively resisting evil and promoting justice. He points to Mahatma Gandhi and Martin Luther King as leaders who have used nonviolent tactics to achieve greater justice and peace.

The pope goes on to identify the family as the "indispensable crucible," in which we "learn to communicate and to show generous concern for one another." In family life we learn to resolve conflicts "not by force but by dialogue, respect, concern for the good of the other, mercy and forgiveness." From the family "the joy of love spills out into the world and radiates in the whole of society." Francis reminds us of Christ, who calls all of us to promote peace in our own circle of influence. We might consider a New Year's resolution to be a peacemaker in our family: ready to apologize for hurting others; prepared to forgive those who have offended us; attending to someone's need to vent or cry; promoting intergenerational dialogue and understanding; keeping spousal conflicts private; and finding creative ways to make Sunday Mass a joyful, unifying experience.

In 2020, Pope Francis linked peace with hope. "Peace is a great and precious value, the object of our hope and the aspiration

---

3. Pope Francis, "Nonviolence: A Style of Politics for Peace," Fiftieth World Day of Peace, January 1, 2017, www.vatican.va.

of the entire human family."[4] The virtue of hope "inspires us and keeps us moving forward, even when obstacles seem insurmountable." The journey of hope demands that we never "encapsulate" others in their misdeeds but "value them for the promise that they embody." Our hope for a better world is based on God's love for us that is liberating, limitless, and tireless and on the power of the Holy Spirit that inspires us to work for justice and peace. This Christian hope can help us deal better with the challenges threatening us today. To keep hope alive we could make a New Year's resolution to find at least one "sign of hope" each day.

*How can we be peacemakers in a world threatened by strife and violence?*

# The Epiphany

On the Feast of the Epiphany, Western Christians remember the visit of the Magi to the child Jesus (see Matt 2:1–12). This story highlights the Christian conviction that Jesus, the long-awaited Jewish Messiah, came to bring salvation to all people, including foreign Gentiles. Matthew, writing to a mixed community of Jewish and Gentile converts, may have wanted to make clear that the Gentiles shared equally in the blessings and mission of Christ. In other words, the liturgical celebration of Epiphany reminds us of the universal thrust of the Christian gospel.

Following the advice of Pope John Paul II, Western Christians can energize our spiritual life by breathing out of both lungs, which involves learning more about the teachings and practices of our Eastern Orthodox brothers and sisters. From the early centuries of Christianity, Eastern and Western Christians developed distinctive theological perspectives and liturgical

---

4. Pope Francis, "Peace as a Journey of Hope," Fifty-third World Day of Peace, January 1, 2020, www.vatican.va.

practices, which, in some cases, caused friction and eventually led to a mutual excommunication in 1054 that remained in effect until it was lifted in 1965 by Pope Paul VI and Patriarch Athenagoras.

In the East, the Feast of the Epiphany originally celebrated both the birth of Jesus and his baptism by John. By the end of the fourth century, however, Eastern Christians separated the two, celebrating Christmas on December 25, as in the Western Church, and the baptism of the Lord on January 6, possibly to Christianize either the winter solstice or a pagan feast. On the Feast of the Epiphany, the Orthodox recall the familiar story of how Jesus came from Galilee to be baptized by John in the Jordan River. Initially John was reluctant, suggesting their roles should be reversed, but he relented when Jesus indicated that they must fulfill all of God's demands. After Jesus was baptized, he saw the Spirit descend like a dove and hover over him and heard a voice from the heavens: "This is my Son, the Beloved, with whom I am well pleased" (Matt 3:17).

The Orthodox see this event not only as the beginning of the public ministry of Jesus but also as a "theophany," the manifestation of the triune God: the Father testifying from on high to the divine Sonship of Jesus; the Son receiving his Father's testimony; the Spirit descending from the Father upon the Son.

The Orthodox emphasis on the baptism of Jesus as a theophany influenced the post–Vatican II revision of our Western liturgical calendar so that our Christmas season now extends past the Epiphany and concludes with the baptism of the Lord on the following Sunday—an extension that makes sense as a celebration of the gradual manifestation of God through the birth and life of Christ.

*How can the Feast of Epiphany overcome the temptation posed by xenophobia?*

# The Communion of Saints

## *Saint Benedict*

On July 11, the Church celebrates the Feast of Saint Benedict of Nursia (480–530), the founder of Western monasticism. According to his biographer, Pope Gregory the Great (d. 604), Benedict studied in Rome but was so upset with the immorality of the culture that he left the city to become a hermit and later founded the monastic community of Monte Cassino, near Naples. It was there that he wrote his famous *Rule*, which has inspired Christian spirituality to this day, especially through well-known contemporary authors like Benedictine sister Joan Chittister and Trappist monk Thomas Merton.

In the prologue to the *Rule*, Benedict states that he intended to prescribe "nothing harsh, nothing burdensome." He did envision his followers seeking God through a disciplined life of prayer and work, based on the conviction that divine grace is present in the ordinary circumstances of daily life. Benedictine spirituality warns against fads and unusual practices while encouraging sensible and humane approaches. We should avoid both spending too much time at work to the neglect of prayer and spending too much time in prayer to the neglect of work responsibilities. All of life's activities should be done in moderation—eating, drinking, sleeping, reading, working, and prayer. Joan Chittister explains: "All must be given its due, but only its due. There should be something of everything and not too much of anything."[5]

Traditionally, Benedictine spirituality has emphasized physical labor that supports sustainable community life and a regular prayer regimen that nourishes the soul, especially the consistent practice of *lectio divina*, which typically involves prayerful reflection on

---

5.   Joan Chittister, *Wisdom Distilled from the Daily: Living the Rule of St. Benedict Today* (San Francisco: HarperOne, 2009), 186.

scripture. A spiritual director gives this advice: Say a prayer and then start reading the Gospel of Luke; when something strikes you, stop and reflect on it for as long as it seems fruitful; then return to reading the text until something else strikes you.

Reflecting on the Benedictine tradition, Thomas Merton declared, "Happiness is not a matter of intensity but of balance and order and rhythm and harmony."[6] As Merton came to realize, his ordered daily prayer life should fuel a passion for justice and peace, reminding us that Benedictine balance and moderation is a catalyst for a passionate involvement in spreading the reign of God in the world.

Christians who appropriated Benedictine spirituality during the pandemic would include people such as sports fans, deprived for months of a usual heavy dose of TV action, who came to realize that they had been spending too much time on the couch and would be better off concentrating on a daily exercise regimen; hard-driving executives who, working at home during the pandemic and interacting more with their families, vowed to make time for them a priority; a collegian spending time at home who decided to reorder his or her life when the university reopened by spending more time studying and less on social media; a Catholic grandmother who was in the habit of going to Mass only periodically when she felt like it committed herself to going every Sunday whether in the mood or not; and teachers who decided to do *lectio divina* at least a couple of times a week over six months.

*How can Benedictine spirituality help us live a balanced life in our fast-paced culture?*

## Saint Patrick

On March 17, the Catholic community celebrates the Feast of Saint Patrick (389–461), the patron saint of Ireland, who

---

6. Thomas Merton, *No Man Is an Island* (San Francisco: HarperOne, 2002), 127.

remains one of the most popular saints even among those who are not Irish. In his mid-teens, Patrick, the son of a public official in Roman Britain, was captured by Irish pirates and held in captivity for six years herding livestock. After these grueling years as a slave, Patrick apparently escaped or was freed, and in an extremely arduous journey made his way back to Britain. Transformed by his horrendous experiences, Patrick did some rudimentary theological studies, was ordained a priest, and around 435 was sent back to Ireland where he became bishop of Armagh. From there, he mounted successful missionary journeys around the country, setting the stage for Ireland to become a predominately Catholic country, which it still is today.

The potato blight that hit Europe in 1845 was especially devastating to the Irish, who were so dependent on potatoes for their daily diet. During the seven-year potato famine in Ireland, an estimated one million died and another two million emigrated. Many traveled to the United States on a miserable month-long voyage where they encountered a strong prejudice that claimed Catholics had a higher allegiance to Rome and could not be good citizens.

Despite these obstacles, Irish immigrants kept coming to the United States—as many as 4.3 million by the 1920s, when stricter immigration laws took effect. Given the discriminatory hiring practices, symbolized by the prevalent sign "Irish need not apply," the early immigrants took the menial jobs they could find, such as cleaning houses and digging canals. The second-generation Irish born in the United States gradually moved up the socio-economic ladder by getting better-paying jobs as teachers and factory workers and by gaining political power, so much so that, by 1900, Irish Catholics were serving as mayors of New York, Boston, and other large cities. This political progress reached a high point in 1960 with the election of John F. Kennedy as the first Catholic president, which signaled the acceptance of Catholics in American society.

The sons of Saint Patrick also gained leadership positions in the U.S. Catholic Church, so that, by 1900, over 60 percent of American bishops were of Irish descent. Among the most influential was Cardinal James Gibbons (1834–1921), the archbishop of Baltimore, who became an advocate for American labor unions and helped convince Pope Leo XIII to support the right of workers to organize in his groundbreaking social encyclical *Rerum Novarum*. The active support of Cardinal Gibbons and many other bishops and pastors for the rights of workers won the respect of various Catholic ethnic groups, each with its own history, saints, and accomplishments.

*What distinctive role can the Catholic community play in developing a viable contemporary spirituality?*

## Saint Joseph

On May 1, the Catholic Church celebrates the Feast of Saint Joseph the Worker, offering a Christian alternative to the annual Communist celebration of International Worker's Day on the same day. The evangelist Matthew calls Joseph a *tekton*, a Greek word that can mean any kind of craftsman, perhaps a stone worker, but traditionally understood as a "carpenter" (see Matt 13:54–57). Regardless, Joseph was a man who worked with his hands and serves as a fitting patron saint of workers.

In 2020, we celebrated the Feast of Joseph the Worker during the pandemic that affected workers around the world and in the United States in diverse ways. By May 2020, some 30 million Americans, over 18 percent of the country's labor force, had filed for unemployment benefits, as businesses had been forced to lay off employees due to stay-at-home orders in states around the country. These startling numbers represent individual human beings who have bills to pay and genuine concerns about the future. For example, Jill, a single mother of two, who has barely stayed afloat for years by working thirty hours a week as a waitress, was grateful for her weekly unemployment check but worried that her restaurant might not be able to reopen.

Millions of other Americans continued to do their jobs despite personal risks: doctors, nurses, police officers, public servants, first responders, and employees in essential businesses. Consider the retired doctor, for instance, who came back to work because she felt called to help in the crisis; a nurse, very fearful he would get infected, who continued to do his best for his patients out of a sense of responsibility; a bus driver, who continued driving his regular route even though some of his passengers did not observe minimal precautions; and a check-out clerk in a grocery store, who kept showing up for work because her need to support her family outweighed the fear of getting sick.

Even workers who stayed at home experienced greater stress: some because they had to care for school-age children who were at home all day; others who were worried about the future of the job market. There were some retired workers who deserved the fruits of their hard work but were deprived of their favorite leisure activities, like interacting with their grandchildren and watching sports on television.

The pandemic reminded many of us how important work is to our spiritual lives. Through meaningful work, we actualize our talents, develop our strengths, earn a living, and find a sense of satisfaction in a job well done. Through our work, we share in God's ongoing creation of the world and contribute to the good of our families, our society, and our world. During the pandemic people honored Joseph the Worker in various ways: praying for the unemployed and those who risked their lives on the job; making the best of isolation by working at home; saying prayers of gratitude for our opportunities to work, often taken for granted;

and maintaining hope that our gracious God will transform, in ways mysterious, the darkness of the pandemic into a brighter future with a more just, equitable, and fulfilling life for all.

*How can Joseph the Worker help us develop an effective spirituality of work in a post-pandemic era?*

# SECULAR CELEBRATIONS

## World Day of Peace

As noted earlier, since 1968, the Catholic Church has been celebrating the World Day of Peace on January 1. Starting with Pope Paul VI, popes have used the occasion to make pronouncements on social issues. Pope Francis begins his 2020 message by describing peace as "a great and precious value, the object of our hope and the aspiration of the entire human family."[7] He sees violence and war as "a form of fratricide that destroys the human family's innate vocation to brotherhood." Peace cannot be built on "fear of mutual destruction or the threat of total annihilation," but only on "a global ethic of solidarity," serving "a future shaped by interdependence and shared responsibility." In order to "break the current dynamic of distrust," we "need to pursue a genuine fraternity based on our common origin from God and exercised in dialogue and mutual trust."[8]

In the second section of his message, Francis mentions the *Hibakusha,* the survivors of the atomic bombing of Hiroshima and Nagasaki, who keep alive the memory of the victims, "so that the conscience of humanity may rise up in the face of every desire for dominance and destruction." The pope reminds us that peace, which "emerges from the human heart," demands

---

7. Pope Francis, "Peace as a Journey of Hope."
8. Pope Francis, "Peace as a Journey of Hope."

"dialogue between men and women who seek the truth beyond ideological and differing opinions." "Listening to one another can lead to mutual understanding and esteem, and even to seeing in an enemy the face of a brother or sister."[9]

In the third section, Francis teaches that "men and women of peace" must resist the temptation "to dominate others" and should follow the teaching of Christ to be generous in forgiving others, who truly are our brothers and sisters. Since "peace permeates every dimension of life in common," the pope goes on to insist that "there can be no true peace unless we show ourselves capable of developing a more just economic system."[10]

After the fourth section on ecological concerns, which notes the violence done to nature and calls for "a peaceful relationship between communities and the land," Pope Francis concludes with a treatment of the virtue of hope as the foundation of peacemaking. Recognizing that "the journey of reconciliation calls for patience and trust," the pope declares that "peace will not be obtained unless it is hoped for." Hope inclines us to believe in the possibility of peace and overcomes the fear that is often the source of conflict. He encourages us "to live in a spirit of universal fraternity, as children of the one heavenly Father," which shatters "the culture of conflict" and can make us "artisans of justice and peace."[11]

*How can we be more creative artisans of peace in the post-pandemic era?*

# Thanksgiving

When we contemplate the secular feast of Thanksgiving from a Christian perspective, there is much truth and value to be

---

9. Pope Francis, "Peace as a Journey of Hope."
10. Pope Francis, "Peace as a Journey of Hope."
11. Pope Francis, "Peace as a Journey of Hope."

celebrated and encouraged. Historically, the celebration has been a genuine response to the perception that we have been blessed by God. In 1621, after a severe winter and first harvest, William Bradford, governor of Plymouth Colony, inaugurated a three-day thanksgiving celebration, which included the Native Americans who had helped the Pilgrims survive. It is, of course, this celebration, with its clear religious message of gratitude to the Supreme Being, that continues to impress itself on the imagination of each succeeding generation of citizens of the United States. When President Washington proclaimed a nationwide day of thanksgiving in 1789, he made it clear that the day should be devoted to prayer and expressions of gratitude to God, and in 1863, President Lincoln invited all citizens to observe the last Thursday of November as a national day of thanksgiving to give "thanks and praise to our beneficent Father who dwellest in the heavens."[12]

Our Thanksgiving celebrations today continue to manifest a great deal of genuine religious sentiment reflecting authentic Christian values. Extended families gather, often at considerable personal sacrifice. Individuals sense that this should be a time of harmony, peace, and reconciliation. The traditional meal becomes a ritual in which family stories are recalled, shared values are celebrated, and hopes for the future are articulated. On this occasion, many people respond generously to the plight of the poor who need food, clothing, and opportunities to help themselves.

The contrast between the noise, busyness, and hype surrounding Christmas and the simpler celebration of Thanksgiving is striking and instructive. Thanksgiving moves at a slower pace, allowing for reflection on blessings received and values treasured. Spared the stress of mandatory gift-giving, we can concentrate on the personal relationships that bring our deepest joys. As Christians,

---

12. President Abraham Lincoln, "Proclamation of Thanksgiving," Washington, DC, October 3, 1863, https://www.abrahamlincolnonline.org/.

we can wholeheartedly affirm the spirit of gratitude, reconciliation, and generosity that surrounds the feast of Thanksgiving.

At the same time, honest reflection on Thanksgiving cannot ignore the gap between those who roam freely through our affluent society and those caught in the hellish circle of poverty. Our faith prompts attention to the needy who live on the margins and miss the safety nets. They are our brothers and sisters, who deserve a chance to take charge of their own destiny. As Christians, we cannot ignore the societal contradictions and the structural injustices that oppress our fellow citizens in this land of abundance.

Thanksgiving is a time to celebrate wholeheartedly our abundant blessings and offer gratitude to God, the Source of all good gifts. We can all enrich our celebration by committing ourselves to assist the less fortunate by supporting, for example, the annual Catholic Campaign for Human Development, which provides, not a handout, but a way out of poverty, a way that empowers more people to share in our national abundance.

*How can we best express our gratitude for the many blessings we enjoy as Americans?*

# Labor Day

During the pandemic, the celebration of Labor Day, traditionally devoted to honoring labor unions and working people, impacted the workforce in various ways.

Bill, a recent college grad, loved his job as a stage designer for a small theater company and looked forward to a career in the theater. When the pandemic closed his theater, he found himself out of a job with time on his hands. As a single guy, he moved back into his parent's home and spent time trying to find another job but to no avail. As the weeks went by, he became more and more anxious that he would never find a job in his field, which led him to seek advice from his parish priest, who advised a daily regimen of prayer and meditation designed to increase trust in God and foster more positive thoughts about the future. Bill was one of many facing emotional problems over their job situation.

Nia, a single Black mother with a young daughter, worked as a checkout cashier in a grocery store, a job she hated but could not quit because she needed to support herself and her child. The virus made it even worse since she went to work fearing for her life. Nia was one of the estimated 15 percent of American workers who were dissatisfied with their jobs even before the pandemic and was one of the millions who could not quit for financial reasons.

Tom owns a restaurant that employed twenty people until he was forced to close for two months because of the virus. During that time, he continued to pay his employees as well as the rent without any revenue. Thanks to the CARES Act passed by Congress in March 2020, Tom was able to get a totally forgivable loan of $55,000 to help him retain his employees during the shutdown and eventually reopened his business on a limited basis.

Jose, who lost his job in a meat processing plant and was unable to pay his rent, was desperately afraid that without a federal moratorium on evictions he and his pregnant wife would become homeless and dependent on relatives.

Lydia, a financial officer with a graduate degree in economics from the University of Chicago, personally fared well during the pandemic, continuing to do her lucrative job from home, as she has for years. She was extremely worried, however, about the more than 40 million persons who lost jobs during the lockdown. Furthermore, her background in economics made her skeptical of a robust job recovery during the pandemic. Personally, Lydia remains extremely grateful that she is among the many Americans who are very satisfied with their current job, and this prompts her to pray for the less fortunate and do whatever she can to assist her furloughed colleagues.

*How can we improve the employment situation in the post-pandemic economy?*

# Independence Day

"We hold these truths to be self-evident, that all men are created equal, that they are endowed by their Creator with certain unalienable Rights, that among these are Life, Liberty and the pursuit of Happiness." This is the most celebrated and significant statement in the Declaration of Independence, adopted by the Second Continental Congress on July 4, 1776. It goes on to list over twenty grievances against King George III to justify to the world community the year-long war being waged by the Thirteen Colonies to achieve independence from Great Britain.

At the urging of John Adams, the Congress chose Thomas Jefferson to write the initial draft of the Declaration. As Jefferson later said, he did not intend to produce an innovative document but to represent "the harmonious sentiment of the day." The idea of God-given human rights was certainly expressed by scholars, journalists, and clergy, in some cases influenced by the British philosopher John Locke (1632–1704), who spoke of the right to "life, liberty and property." With the help of a committee of editors who, according to Jefferson, "mangled" his text, the final document included the absolutely crucial notion that human beings are "endowed by their Creator" with certain rights. We have rights, not from the government or from common custom, but from God, which guarantees they are truly "unalienable." The Declaration also has two other references to God: "appealing to the Supreme Judge of the world for the rectitude of our intentions"; its closing line firmly cements the spirt of the occasion, "with a firm reliance on the protection of Divine Providence, we mutually pledge to each other our Lives, our Fortunes, and our sacred Honor."

Critics of the Declaration immediately seized on the obvious contradiction between professing the equality of all people and the prevalent institution of slavery in the colonies, a contradiction between ideals and practice that continues to plague our nation today. One way to redeem the Declaration is to see it as an aspirational document that continually prompts us to do our best to live up to our highest national ideals while recognizing that our search for perfection is always beyond our grasp.

Historically, the Declaration has functioned in this constructive way. The nineteenth-century abolitionists commonly used the phrase "all men are created equal" to advocate for the freedom of slaves denied their fundamental human rights. The women's suffrage movement, going back into the early nineteenth century, argued that women had an unalienable right to vote and made use of the slogan "all men and women are created equal." Abraham Lincoln, who often drew on the aspirational ideals of the Declaration, linked his political positions to "the sentiments embodied" in that "notable instrument," which, as he put it in his famous Gettysburg Address, "brought forth, on this continent, a new nation, conceived in Liberty." Martin Luther King, who regularly called on both our founding documents and the Christian scriptures in his appeal for justice, insisted that the architects of the Declaration signed "a promissory note to which every American was to fall heir." In the post-pandemic era, we can continue to draw on the fundamental truths enunciated by the Declaration of Independence to guide us in the ongoing quest for a more just society and more perfect union.

*What can we do to promote the ideals enunciated by our Founding Fathers in our society distrustful of government and social institutions?*

# Earth Day

On April 22, 2020—during the pandemic—we celebrated the fiftieth anniversary of the annual Earth Day dedicated to saving our planet. To prepare for that year's celebration, activists in 190 countries sponsored a series of coordinated activities: collecting data to measure air and water quality; cleaning up neighborhoods, beaches, and parks; planting 7.8 billion trees, one for every human on earth; and educating students and leaders on the dangers of climate change. It was of special concern in 2020 that the United States was in the formal year-long process of withdrawing from the Paris climate agreement, signed by two hundred countries on Earth Day in 2015.

Thanks to the groundbreaking encyclical of Pope Francis, *Laudato Si'* (*On Care for Our Common Home*), environmental concerns are now an integral part of Catholic Social Teaching. After consulting with eminent scientists, Francis affirmed that human activity, mainly the burning of fossil fuels, contributes to climate change, which is "one of the principal challenges facing humanity in our age" (*Laudato Si'* 23–24). The pope, who draws a close connection between the damage done to the earth and the suffering inflicted on the poor, called for urgent action to reduce carbon emissions and slow global warming.

Pope Francis believes the Christian tradition has resources that can help us protect our common home. We are embodied spirits who are organically related to the earth. Our calling is not to dominate and subdue the material world but to respect it as a gift from God by being good stewards of the earth. As Francis notes, "Rather than a problem to be solved, the world is a joyful mystery to be contemplated with gladness and joy" (*LS* 12). As Christians, we remember that the Son of God came to our earth and shared our existence. He delighted in nature and drew lessons from the birds of the air and the lilies of the field. As members of "a sublime communion joined by unseen hands," we have a moral obligation to preserve the earth from harm so that it will be available for the next generation as a source of sustenance and delight.

Our faith teaches us that we find happiness not by accumulating material goods but by forming loving relationships with our God, our families, our neighbors, and our earth. In this regard, the pope notes, "The emptier a person's heart is, the more he or she needs things to buy, own and consume" (*LS*, 204). Catholic Social Teaching insists that economic policies should not be driven by greed, which benefits the wealthy, but by concern for the common good, which includes justice for all and care for the earth. Given the gravity of our environmental crisis, Francis encourages all of us to examine our lifestyle and our priorities. He insists that purchasing is always a moral act and not simply an economic activity. He encourages us to simplify our lifestyle by, for example, "avoiding the use of plastic, reducing water consumption, separating refuse, using public transportation or carpooling, planting trees, and turning off unnecessary lights." Finally, Pope Francis reminds us of the importance of prayer in managing this crisis: "All-powerful God, bring healing to our lives, that we may protect the world and not prey on it. That we may sow beauty, not pollution and destruction."[13]

*How can we protect our common home that is threatened by climate change?*

---

13. Pope Francis, "World Day of Prayer for the Care of Creation," September 1, 2015, www.vatican.va.

# 7

## Spiritual Mentors

The *Catechism* teaches that "all Christians in any state or walk of life are called to the fullness of Christian life and to the perfection of charity....The holiness of the People of God will grow in fruitful abundance, as is clearly shown in the history of the Church through the lives of so many saints" (§2013).

The *Catechism* further states that "the witnesses who have preceded us into the kingdom, especially those whom the Church recognizes as saints, share in the living tradition of prayer by the example of their lives, the transmission of their writings, and their prayer today" (§2683). It also states that is "by canonizing some of the faithful, i.e., by solemnly proclaiming that they practiced heroic virtue and lived in fidelity to God's grace, the Church recognizes the power of the Spirit of holiness within her and sustains the hope of believers by proposing the saints to them as models and intercessors. The saints have always been the source and origin of renewal in the most difficult moments in the Church's history" (§828).

# MARY OF NAZARETH

In our effort to develop a post-pandemic spirituality, we can look to Mary of Nazareth for inspiration and guidance. The Gospel of Luke's account of the annunciation (Luke 1:26–38) portrays a conversation between the angel Gabriel and a young Jewish woman, Mary, leading to her consent to be the mother of the promised Messiah. In her excellent book on Mary, *Truly Our Sister*, theologian Elizabeth Johnson offers a scholarly interpretation of this story, highlighting Mary's active role as a hearer and doer of God's word. Luke's story follows the literary pattern of other stories of the commissioning of the great Hebrew prophets, like Moses and Jeremiah. The angel Gabriel greets Mary; she is troubled, and Gabriel tells her not to be afraid; the angel goes on to explain she will conceive a son who will be called "Son of the Most High" and who will receive the everlasting throne of King David. Mary asks how this can be since she has not yet moved in with her husband Joseph; Gabriel explains that this will be the work of the Holy Spirit and, as a sign that "nothing is impossible for God," informs Mary that her older relative Elizabeth is six months pregnant; Mary responds, "Here am I, the servant of the Lord; let it be with me according to your word" (Luke 1:38).

Johnson notes that Luke makes the hero of the story a young, uneducated Galilean peasant living in the small village of Nazareth, with a population between three hundred and four hundred, in the region of Galilee. Though in her early teens, Mary was not a "teenager" in our sense of the word. She was a young woman, already married, capable of bearing children and able to make a thoughtful, mature decision about following God's will.

By framing the story of the annunciation as a prophetic call, Luke gives Mary a crucial public role in the history of Israel. Her yes to God sets her off on a life journey into an unknown future, sustained by God in good times and bad. It heralds a new era in

God's grand plan to make Israel a light to the nations. Her son, Jesus, will proclaim the divine plan to save all people and, by his death and resurrection, will make it definitive and irrevocable. In Luke's account, Gabriel tells Mary that the Holy Spirit will "come upon" her and "overshadow" her. This does not really provide a clear answer to her question about getting pregnant. Nor does it mean that the Spirit mated with Mary. It does mean that the Spirit drew near to Mary in an intimate relationship, as the Source of life, guidance, protection, and hope.

It is remarkable that Luke, writing in a patriarchal culture, not only makes Mary the protagonist of his story but highlights her mature, independent, and thoughtful consent. She does not consult with any male figure or seek their permission but acts decisively as her own person out of her profound trust in the God of her people. Empowered by the Spirit, she remains faithful to her vocation by visiting her pregnant relative, Elizabeth; enlivening the wedding reception at Cana; enduring her son's cruel death on Calvary; and rejoicing with the disciples at Pentecost.

In coping with the challenges of the contemporary world, we can find inspiration in the life of our sister Mary—her faith, strength, wisdom, courage, and role as the "hope of our darkened ways,"[1] as the Jesuit poet Gerard Manley Hopkins wrote.

*How can Mary help us meet the challenges and seize the opportunities we encounter on our spiritual journey?*

# JOSEPH OF NAZARETH

In developing a contemporary spirituality, let us reflect on Joseph of Nazareth, who plays a major role in Matthew's infancy account. Joseph was a woodworker in the small town of Naza-

---

1. Gerard Manley Hopkins, "Ad Mariam," https://www.poetrynook.com/poem/ad-mariam.

reth in Galilee, a region under the control of the puppet king, Herod Antipas. The story in Matthew notes that Joseph is married to Mary, but they are not yet living together. He finds out that Mary is pregnant. Perplexed, he can only assume rape or infidelity. Being "an upright man," Joseph does not want to expose Mary to public ridicule or the harsh punishment of the Jewish law, so he decides to divorce her quietly. At this point, the angel of the Lord appears to him in a dream, explaining that the pregnancy is the work of the Holy Spirit and telling him not to fear taking Mary into his home. Furthermore, the angel commissions Joseph to name the baby Jesus. When Joseph awakes, he acts quickly and decisively, bringing Mary into his home.

We read in Matthew's account that astrologers from the east arrive in Bethlehem, bringing gifts of gold, frankincense, and myrrh to the newborn king of the Jews. The Magi followed a star that led them to the devious King Herod in Jerusalem. With the advice of scholars, he sent them to Bethlehem to get detailed information about the child so that he could also go pay him homage. His real intent, as Matthew makes clear, was to destroy this potential threat to his throne. After paying homage to Jesus, the astrologers were warned in a dream not to report to Herod, so they returned to their native land by another route.

After the Magi left, the angel of the Lord again spoke to Joseph in a dream, telling him to take Mary and Jesus to Egypt to escape the murderous designs of Herod. Matthew tells us the cruel king murdered all the male children "in and around Bethlehem" who were "two years old or under," based on when the astrologers had first seen the star. That very night, Joseph took his wife and son to Egypt, where they stayed until Herod died. Once again guided by angelic messages in his dreams, Joseph and his family returned to Israel, settling in Nazareth.

Joseph inspires us to stay alert to the various ways God speaks to us and to respond decisively to the divine call. We can imagine individuals following the good example of Joseph. Consider, for example, a man who helped a neighbor in need after hearing a homily on seeing Christ in the poor; a woman who accepted God's forgiveness after reading the story of the prodigal son; a husband who became more attentive to his wife after she criticized him for being self-centered; the community organizer who rededicated herself to her work, inspired by a mother working two jobs to support herself and her baby; a grandmother who cut back on gossiping after going to confession; the Catholic who stopped using racist language after befriending a Black neighbor; and the family who started getting along better after a joyful celebration of Mass on Christmas Eve. God does indeed speak to us in and through our ordinary experience.

*How can the good example of Joseph help us develop a realistic spirituality?*

# JOHN THE BAPTIST

The social isolation imposed by the recent pandemic intensified the loneliness that many Americans already experience, with adverse impacts on mental health, including depression and anxiety. Facing this problem, some Christians found inspiration in the life of John the Baptist. In the New Testament, we first hear of John as the son born to Zechariah and Elizabeth in their old age (see Luke 1:13–17). Decades later, in the fifteenth year of the reign of Tiberius Caesar, when Pilate was governor of Judea and Herod Antipas ruled Galilee, John appeared in the wilderness of Judea by the Jordan River preaching a baptism of repentance for the forgiveness of sins. He reminded people of the great prophet Elijah, wearing camel's hair garments and eating locusts and wild honey. He had clear, pointed messages for the multitudes who came to him. He called the Pharisees and Sadducees a "brood of vipers" and admonished them to repent and bear fruit. Individuals with two coats and enough food should share with the less fortunate. Tax collectors should be fair, and soldiers should not violently rob people (see Luke 3:10–18).

When Jesus came from Nazareth in Galilee to be baptized, John was reluctant but consented when Jesus insisted it was necessary "to fulfill all righteousness" (Matt 3:15). John, who enjoyed a large following himself, humbly turned leadership of the reform movement over to Jesus, God's Chosen One and the "Lamb of God" (John 1:29–34).

Sometime before Jesus began his own public ministry, John publicly chastised Herod for marrying his brother's wife, Herodias, an adulterous and incestuous relationship. At the urging of Herodias, Herod had John arrested, put in chains, and imprisoned (see Matt 14:3–12). While in prison, John apparently began to doubt his faith in Jesus and sent a message to him asking if he is in fact the Messiah or "should we look for another." Jesus responds by proclaiming that in his ministry, the prophecy of Isaiah is being fulfilled—the blind will see, the crippled will walk, lepers are cured, the deaf shall hear, the dead will rise, and the poor will receive the good news. Jesus later extolled John as the new Elijah and the greatest of human beings (see Matt 11:2–13). We can imagine John going to his death at the hands of Herod and his vengeful wife strengthened and enlightened by the assuring deeds and words of Jesus, God's Chosen One.

It is instructive to reflect on the life of John the Baptist, especially that a man of such courage, discipline, and conviction fell into confusion and doubt under the constraints of prison. It is not surprising that many of us had difficulty coping with the isolation imposed by the pandemic. Through the eyes of faith, however, it was an opportunity to deepen our reliance on Christ—our brother, friend, and companion—who walks the path with us, though often unnoticed and unrecognized. The isolation that diminished our lives also offered more time for reflection and prayer that reached out to Christ, seeking his assurance and sharpening our awareness of his abiding presence.

Strengthened by Christ, some people found creative ways to make supportive connections with others by sharing, for example, more intimate conversations and communal prayer with household members, making periodic virtual contact with separated family members, taking walks outside with a friend while masked, hosting a few friends for a meal outside while carefully distanced, and making at least some minimal connection with parishioners by streaming Sunday liturgies. Guided by John the Baptist, faithful people transformed the cross of the pandemic into a deeper and more effective faith in the risen Christ.

*How can John the Baptist help us develop a viable spirituality that can manage the distinctive challenges of today's world?*

# THOMAS AQUINAS (1224/25–1274)

Thomas Aquinas, celebrated on January 28 as a saint and doctor of the Church, was not only one of the greatest theologians in the history of the Church but also a holy man who persevered in his vocation and mission despite serious challenges. He can serve as a guide to a spirituality that is grounded in a solid theology and is open to new developments.

Thomas was born into an aristocratic family in 1224 or 1225 near Aquino, which is midway between Rome and Naples. When he was around the age of five, his parents sent him to the great Benedictine monastery of Monte Cassino, no doubt hoping that this would put him on a path to a prestigious and lucrative career as an abbot. In 1239, Thomas was transferred to the University of Naples, where he came under the influence of Dominican preachers and teachers. At age nineteen, Thomas made the radical decision to renounce the career path planned by his parents and join the newly established Dominican Order devoted to preaching the gospel. This so upset his mother, Theodora, that she had Thomas kidnapped and brought home by two of her sons, where she kept him imprisoned for a year in a desperate, but unsuccessful, effort to reprogram his deviant thinking. After escaping, with the tacit agreement of his mother, Thomas, staying true to his calling, joined the Dominicans and was a faithful friar the rest of his life.

The young Dominican then resumed his studies, first under Saint Albert the Great at Cologne and later at the University of Paris, where he completed a degree and took up a teaching post in 1256. The great theological issue of the day was the general relationship between faith and reason and, more specifically, how to deal with the rediscovery of the philosophy of Aristotle that was lost in the Christian West but was kept alive by Islamic scholars. Some Christian thinkers opposed Aristotle's philosophy as a threat to the faith. Others, including Thomas, argued that both faith and reason are united in a search for the truth and that Christian theology could be enriched by dialogue with Aristotle's philosophy.

Out of his dialogue with Aristotle and many Christian scholars, especially Augustine, Thomas produced his magnificent synthesis, known by its Latin title, *Summa Theologiae*, a classic work considered a paradigm of Catholic orthodox theology. It is important to remember that in his day Thomas was an innovator, open to new ideas, unafraid of dialogue, and dedicated to making the faith relevant to the changing world. Throughout his academic career, his innovative approach generated a strong backlash. For example, he needed police protection from angry protestors at his inaugural lecture at the University of Paris, and, in 1270, just a few years before Thomas's death, the archbishop of

Paris condemned some teachings of Aristotle that could be used to attack Thomas.

Despite such criticism, Thomas poured himself into his ministry as a theologian for twenty-five years of truly prodigious daily effort, lecturing, writing, editing, sometimes dictating to more than one secretary at a time, and producing numerous books, articles, commentaries, sermons, letters, and prayers. He maintained this frenetic pace until December 6, 1273, when he suddenly stopped working after a deep mystical experience during his usual morning Mass that left him feeling that all he had written was like straw. He died months later, on March 7, 1274, leaving his great *Summa* incomplete but persevering to the end in fidelity to his vocation. Thomas Aquinas not only developed a classic theology with enduring value but also left us a striking personal story that can inspire us to remain faithful to our own vocation and mission in today's challenging situations.

*How can Aquinas help us to remain faithful to our personal vocation?*

# MATTEO RICCI (1552–1610)

The great Jesuit missionary to China, Matteo Ricci, the oldest of thirteen children, went to Rome to study law but decided to join the Jesuits and was ordained in 1580. Driven by his desire to preach the gospel in China, he became fluent in Chinese and, in 1583, gained entrance to a country with a deep distrust of and disdain for foreigners. He gradually earned the respect of Chinese scholars (*literati*) by his prodigious memory and subtle understanding of the Confucian classics, well-known to all public servants. In 1601, he fulfilled his great dream of reaching the capital city of Peking, where he gained the attention of the emperor, who provided him with a residence and frequently sent him questions about Western ways and accomplishments, such as clocks and maps. When Ricci died on May 11, 1610, the emperor provided him with an impressive burial site located on the outskirts of Beijing and where visitors today can still pay their respects to the great missionary.

By a careful study of the classic Confucian works, such as the *Analects* and *Doctrine of the Mean*, Ricci was convinced that nothing in these texts contradicted Christianity. He came to see K'ung Fu'tzu (Ricci gave him the Latin name Confucius) as the holiest of all the wise teachers and his moral philosophy as a helpful preparation for the gospel. He identified the "Lord of Heaven" mentioned in the classics with the one God worshiped by Christians and noted the Confucian belief in an afterlife of reward and punishment.

Ricci began writing books in Chinese, including a catechism, which contained a simple explanation of the Christian faith, and his most important work, *The True Meaning of the Lord of Heaven*, which demonstrated the essential compatibility of Confucianism and Christianity. He also developed an indigenous liturgy that incorporated the annual rites honoring Confucius and the common practice of venerating ancestors as permissible ways of honoring the dead.

By the time Ricci died, there were thousands of Chinese converts to Christianity, and the stage was set for many more. At the end of the seventeenth century, there were about three hundred thousand Christians in China. In 1692, the Emperor K'ang Hsi even issued an edict of tolerance allowing Christian missionaries to preach publicly. Ricci's adaptation strategy had worked, and his dream of a Christian China was primed for fulfillment.

That dream evaporated, however, on November 13, 1704, when Pope Clement XI, faced with objections from cardinals unfamiliar with China, decreed that Chinese Christians could not practice the traditional veneration of ancestors. The emperor was incensed and effectively dismantled the missionary base Ricci had established. This decision, which stood until 1939 when Pope Pius XII approved the Chinese rites, was surely one of the most consequential decisions ever made by Rome, effectively relegating Chinese Catholics to a tiny minority of the most populous country in the world, then and now.

The story of Matteo Ricci prompts further thoughts. Jesus Christ has universal significance, and his gospel can enrich all cultures. As baptized Christians, we all have a vocation to be a missionary in our circle of influence. We cannot control the results of our efforts to share our faith with others, but we can hope that God blesses our efforts: for example, parents who have been unsuccessful in handing on the practice of their religious tradition to their children can hope that their efforts have made a difference and that their offspring remain in the embrace of the Gracious Mystery.

*How can the story of Matteo Ricci help us overcome xenophobia and develop a more inclusive contemporary spiritualty?*

# AUGUSTUS TOLTON (1854–1897)

Augustus Tolton, a former slave, was the first Black priest in the United States. Augustus was born in 1854, the second son of Martha and Peter Tolton, a married couple held in slavery in Missouri. As practicing Catholics, they had their son baptized, and his godmother, the slave owner's wife, saw to his religious education. When Augustus was seven, his mother led him and his two siblings to freedom in Quincy, Illinois.

In his early years of freedom, Augustus felt a call to become a priest. He found support in his vocation from Father Peter McGiff, pastor of Saint Boniface Parish, who allowed him to attend the parish school. This created such a backlash from the white parents, however, who threatened to withdraw their children and withhold financial support, that Martha agreed to take him out of the school. Still determined to follow his vocation, Augustus pursued a makeshift education with the help of some Franciscan priests, who enabled him to make informal use of the resources of their local college, Saint Francis. The young man took this opportunity to learn Greek and Latin as part of his preparation for the seminary. Sadly, however, no seminary in the United States would accept a Black candidate for the priesthood. Undaunted, he gained acceptance in the prestigious Pontifical College for the Propagation of the Faith in Rome, which prepared priests for missionary work. He completed his studies in six years and was ordained a priest in 1886.

Instead of being assigned as a missionary in Africa, as expected, Vatican officials sent him back to Quincy to serve as pastor of Saint Joseph Church, a designated Black parish, making him the first Roman Catholic pastor in the United States publicly known to be Black. Tolton gave himself in service to his people, building up the parish and attracting to his Masses large crowds, including white Catholics drawn by his engaging sermons and beautiful singing of the Latin liturgy. At the same time, he had to endure a good deal of prejudice and bigotry as well as clerical envy that included racial slurs repeated by a neighboring pastor.

In 1889, when Augustus was feeling increasingly alone and despondent, Archbishop Patrick Fehan called him to Chicago to serve Black Catholics in his diocese. After making helpful contacts, Tolton established Saint Monica Catholic Parish on the southside of Chicago in 1891. Soon, the original group of some thirty Black parishioners grew to over six hundred, including white Catholics attracted by his charismatic leadership. Needing financial help to build a larger church, Tolton travelled around the country making the case that the Church should provide a welcoming home for Black Catholics.

His dedicated service to Black Catholics earned him national recognition. For example, he was invited to participate in the 1889 centenary celebration of the establishment of the first U.S. Catholic diocese in Baltimore. Newspaper accounts at the time noted the striking image of a lone Black priest at the altar with the many prominent white clergymen.

Sadly, Augustus Tolton died suddenly in 1897 at the age of forty-three with so much more to do for his parish and the American church. His funeral attracted a large crowd, including hundreds of priests who had grown to respect him. Recently, in 2019, Pope Francis advanced his cause for canonization by declaring him "Venerable," the last step before beatifying him and declaring him a saint of the Church.

*How can the life story of Augustus Tolton help the Church become a more credible advocate for racial justice?*

# THEA BOWMAN (1937–1990)

Thea Bowman, a Black vowed religious woman, teacher, scholar, and gifted public speaker, explored in depth what it means to be Catholic and African American in the United States. Thea, the daughter of a physician and a teacher, grew up in Canton, Mississippi, where she personally experienced the indignities of institutionalized segregation. Aware of the financial limitations of Canton's Black public school, her Methodist parents sent her to a local Catholic school, Holy Child Jesus, where she felt respected and loved by her dedicated teachers. Impressed with what she later called the school's "grace-filled environment," the young nine-year-old girl, with her parent's permission, joined the Catholic Church. When she was fifteen, she moved to La Crosse, Wisconsin, to start the process of becoming the first Black member of the Franciscan Sisters of Perpetual Adoration, which remained her supportive community for the rest of her life. At the direction of her community, she taught elementary school in La Crosse and high school at Christ Child in her hometown.

To enrich her teaching ministry, she took classes at Catholic University of America (CUA) in Washington, DC. In 1972, she completed a doctorate in English literature with a dissertation on Thomas More's 1534 A *Dialogue of Comfort against Tribulation*, which emphasized the importance of emotion in effective communication. From 1972 to 1978, she taught classes at CUA and Viterbo College in La Crosse, Wisconsin.

In 1978, Thea was appointed director of the Office of Intercultural Affairs for the Diocese of Jackson, Mississippi. That position enabled her to integrate the experience of Black Catholics into the life of the Catholic Church by helping found the Institute for Black Catholic Studies at Xavier University in New Orleans; playing a major role in producing an African American Catholic hymnal, with "soulful songs" that are holistic, participatory, realistic, spirit-filled, and life-giving; writing a handbook for those ministering in Black communities, stressing the need to listen to the people and learn from them; assisting in the establishment of the National Black Sisters' Conference; and traveling extensively around the country promoting inclusion of Black spirituality into the life of the whole Catholic community. She was a charismatic speaker, who employed vivid imagery, rhythmic speech patterns, bodily gestures, and familiar songs in her inspiring presentations. Despite developing breast cancer in 1984, she continued her busy schedule, always with joy in her heart and a smile on her face.

On June 2, 1989, Thea addressed the full body of the American bishops at their annual meeting at Seton Hall University in East Orange, New Jersey.[2] Seated in a wheelchair because her cancer had spread to her bones, she spoke to the bishops "heart

---

2. Subcommittee on African American Affairs, "Sr. Thea Bowman's Address to the U.S. Bishop's Conference," USCCB, June 1989, https://www.usccb.org.

to heart" as her brothers, asking them to help her find her "true home" in the Church, according to Christ's will. Addressing the sin of slavery, she highlighted the many achievements of African culture as well as the resilience and creativity of the African slaves, who helped build the country and continue to suffer from discrimination. She noted how Catholic education helped people like her find a home in the Church and urged the bishops to provide greater support for this ministry so that Black Catholics could evangelize themselves.

Thea told the bishops that she and other Black Catholics came to the Church "fully functioning," bringing their contemplative, biblical, holistic, integrated, joyful, and communal Black spirituality, which, she warned, just might shout out, "Amen, Hallelujah, Thank you, Jesus," in the middle of one of their sermons. She reminded the bishops that their job is to "enable" God's people to do the Church's work of teaching, preaching, witnessing, worshiping, serving, healing, and reconciling in the modern world.

To promote a "multi-cultured Church," Black Catholics have to overcome apathy and inertia by realizing the richness of their heritage and accepting their proper responsibility as active participants in the life of the Church. They must be included from the very beginning in the normal process of pastoral planning.

Thea concluded her inspiring presentation with a plea to the bishops to "walk together" so that we can be "truly Catholic," overcoming poverty, loneliness, and alienation and building a "holy city" where they will know "we are here because we love one another." With that, she got the assembled bishops to stand up, cross their arms, and join her in singing the familiar civil rights anthem "We Shall Overcome."

A few weeks before she died on March 30, 1990, at the age of fifty-two, Thea Bowman offered this prayer: "We unite ourselves with Christ's redemptive work when we reconcile, when we make peace, when we share the good news that God is in our lives, when we reflect to our brothers and sisters God's healing, God's unconditional love." Since her death, she has been memorialized in many ways, including books, films, buildings, institutions, plays, and works of art. Her talks—available on YouTube—help us to experience her vibrant spirit. Today, she is properly called a "Servant of God," as her canonization process continues.

*How can the spirit and message of Thea Bowman help the Catholic Church be a better witness to racial equality in today's world?*

# DOROTHY DAY (1897–1980)

Best known as the founder of the Catholic Worker Movement, Dorothy Day, as a young woman, participated in the historic struggle for women's suffrage. Day was born on November 8, 1897, in Brooklyn and, as a youngster, moved first to Oakland, California, and then to Chicago. An avid reader, she attended the University of Illinois, majoring in journalism, but dropped out after two years and moved to New York, where she worked for several socialist publications. After a couple of years, she moved to Washington, DC, to work with the National Woman's Party, dedicated to women's suffrage.

By 1916, nine states had granted women the right to vote, but Woodrow Wilson, who served as president from 1913 to 1921, opposed a federal amendment guaranteeing suffrage for all women. Starting in January 1917, suffragists, known as "Silent Sentinels," began, in an unprecedented strategy, picketing the White House; wearing purple, white, and gold sashes; and holding signs pressuring Wilson to support their cause. At first, the president tolerated the protests, but after the United States entered World War I in April 1917, he, along with many others, considered the picketing to be unpatriotic.

On November 10, 1917, Dorothy Day and thirty-two other suffragists were arrested for peacefully protesting outside the White House and taken to the Occoquan Workhouse, where they were imprisoned and brutally treated in what is known as the "Night of Terror." News reports based on one woman's recollection stressed police brutality: handcuffing one woman to the bars of her cell so she had to stand all night; throwing another into her cell so hard she was rendered unconscious; failing to treat a woman who had a heart attack; and slamming Dorothy Day twice against an iron bench. In her autobiography, *The Long Loneliness*, Dorothy noted that their treatment was rough and demeaning but not as bad as the news reports. She emphasized the hardships of the ten-day hunger strike that she and the others voluntarily undertook, leading to physical exhaustion and nausea, emotional distress, and fear, as well as deeper feelings of desolation and futility. A few weeks after ending their hunger strike, the women were released from jail and later pardoned. Dorothy Day may not have been as passionate about women's suffrage as her companions, nor did she regularly join their ongoing protests, but she did participate with conviction and courage in one of the crucial events that led to the right of women to vote.

Within months of the Night of Terror, President Wilson reversed his position and began to encourage Congress to act on the federal suffrage amendment that had been first introduced in the late nineteenth century. Meanwhile, committed suffragists continued their public protests, leading to more arrests and hunger strikes designed to put pressure on legislators. After the Senate failed to pass the suffrage amendment in 1918, it was reintroduced in 1919 and was passed by the House and the Senate, sending it to the states for ratification. By March 1920, a total of thirty-five states had approved the amendment, one shy of the three-fourths needed. By August 18, 1920, seven southern states had already rejected it, leaving the fate of women's suffrage in the hands of Tennessee. Their state Senate approved it, but the House was evenly divided until a twenty-four-year-old representative, previously opposed, changed his mind at the urging of his mother and voted for it, thus guaranteeing women the right to vote after a long, hard struggle.

*How can the courageous example of Dorothy Day inspire our ongoing struggle against patriarchy and sexism?*

# ELIZABETH CADY STANTON (1815–1902)

The social activist and ardent abolitionist Elizabeth Cady Stanton played an important role in the women's suffrage movement that eventually led to the Nineteenth Amendment guaranteeing women the right to vote in 1920. The daughter of a federal judge, David Cady, Elizabeth managed to get an education despite the prevalent patriarchal limitations. At age twenty-five, she married the journalist and later lawyer Henry Stanton, the father of her seven children and marital partner for forty-seven years until his death in 1887.

From her early years, Elizabeth was passionate about social causes, especially the abolitionist and temperance movements. Her interest in women's issues was broad, including educational equality, expanded employment opportunities, gender-neutral divorce laws, and the right to serve on juries as well as women's suffrage. In her personal life, she experienced sexism that influenced her public positions. As an eleven-year-old, she tried to comfort her father grieving the death of her brother, prompting the reply: "Oh my daughter, I wish you were a boy." After graduating from a local academy with good grades, she was upset that her less-gifted male classmates were able to enroll in Union College, which did not accept women. For her Christian wedding, she insisted that the odious phrase "promise to obey" be deleted from the vows. Although a committed abolitionist, she was not allowed to speak at the 1840 World Anti-Slavery Convention in London but was forced to listen in silence from the spectators' gallery.

At the historic Seneca Falls Convention in 1848, Stanton delivered a speech titled "Declaration of Sentiments," which contained paraphrases of the Declaration of Independence: "All men and women are created equal." Women suffering "a long train of abuses" must "demand the equal station to which they are entitled." The "absolute tyranny" of men over women has deprived them of the "elective franchise," forced them to "promise obedience to their husbands," denied them "the avenues to wealth and distinction," and excluded them "from the ministry." Using singular pronouns in her indictment of patriarchy, she declared: "He has endeavored, in every way that he could, to destroy her confidence in her own powers, to lessen her self-respect, and to make her willing to lead a dependent and abject life." "In view of this entire disenfranchisement of one-half the people of this country," she insisted that "women have immediate admission to all the rights and privileges which belong to them as citizens of the United States." Elizabeth spent the rest of her life trying to implement the goals of her eloquent declaration.

In 1851, Stanton began a lifelong, mutually enriching, and emotionally fulfilling friendship with Susan B. Anthony, as well as a collaborative working partnership, in which Elizabeth served as a mentor and speech writer and Susan as a strategist and organizer. Elizabeth found a vehicle for disseminating her views in a woman's newspaper, *The Revolution*, which she helped establish. She also helped found the National Woman Suffrage Association, which was a major voice for women's rights, including a constitutional amendment to guarantee the franchise for women. In her zeal for women's rights, Stanton vigorously opposed the Fifteenth Amendment granting voting rights to Black males because it did not include women. Unfortunately, she resorted to racial slurs and stereotypes to bolster her case.

Late in her life, Elizabeth published *The Women's Bible*, an effort to expose the sexist bias in the Bible, which dismayed many suffragists, including Anthony. Somewhat marginalized from the suffragist movement and in poor health, Elizabeth Cady Stanton spent her last years at her home in New York City, where she died in 1902, almost two decades before her dream of women's suffrage became a reality in 1920.

*How can the example of Elizabeth Cady Stanton help us in the ongoing quest for gender equality?*

# SUSAN B. ANTHONY (1820–1906)

On November 1, 1872, a fifty-two-year-old Quaker woman living in Rochester, New York, went to a voter registration office in a local barber shop with her three sisters and convinced the election inspectors to allow them to register to vote in the upcoming presidential election. Four days later, on November 5, 1872, she and fourteen suffragists cast ballots in the presidential election won by the incumbent Ulysses Grant. For breaking the law forbidding women to vote, she was arrested, subjected to a sham trial in a federal district court, which did not allow jury deliberation, found guilty, fined a hundred dollars that she refused to pay, and released without serving jail time.

During her trial, Susan B. Anthony gave an impassioned speech advocating the right of women to vote. Invoking the preamble of the Constitution, she argued that by voting she did not commit a crime but simply exercised her citizen's rights. She declared, "It was we, the people; not we the white male citizens" who formed the Union to secure the blessings of liberty "to the whole people—women as well as men." To disenfranchised women, the government is a "hateful oligarchy of sex," which "ordains all men sovereigns, all women subjects," and "carries dissension, discord, and rebellion into every home of the nation." It is "a downright mockery" to speak to women about the "blessings of liberty" while they are denied "the ballot," the "only means" of securing those blessings. "The disenfranchisement of one entire half of the people" is "a violation of the supreme law of the land." Having established that women are truly persons and citizens with equal rights, Anthony concluded that "every discrimination against women in the constitutions and laws of the several states is today null and void."

The well-publicized trial of Susan B. Anthony made women's suffrage a prominent national issue and fueled an intense effort to secure voting rights through the court system. In 1875, however, the Supreme Court put an end to this strategy by ruling that "the Constitution of the United States does not confer the right of suffrage upon anyone." As a result, Anthony led the way in advocating for women's suffrage through a federal constitutional amendment. Though a lifelong proponent of Black rights, she opposed the Fifteenth Amendment of 1870 granting suffrage to Black men because it did not include women. In 1878, she succeeded in getting a women's suffrage amendment introduced in Congress.

As a single woman, she was able to travel throughout the country advocating women's rights, especially to vote. Blessed with great organizational skills, she helped merge two suffragist groups into the National American Woman Suffrage Association, which she helped lead from 1890 to 1900. Her strong Quaker faith in the equality of all people enabled her to persevere in the cause, even when subjected to great criticism, especially that she was "destroying the foundation of marriage." Nevertheless, her perseverance earned the admiration of many, including President McKinley, who hosted her eightieth birthday in the White House six years before her death in 1906. It was on August 26, 1920, that the so-called Anthony Amendment, originally introduced in 1878, was officially adopted, guaranteeing the right of women to vote. Recalling that historic achievement over a century ago invites grateful reflection on the great contributions of Susan B. Anthony and so many other dedicated persons who helped create the more just society women and men enjoy today.

*What can we learn from Susan B. Anthony about participating in the political process in our polarized society?*

# JACKIE ROBINSON (1914–1972)

On April 15, 1947, the twenty-eight-year-old Jackie Robinson played first base for the Brooklyn Dodgers at Ebbets Field, becoming the first African American to break the unofficial color barrier that had kept baseball totally segregated for more than fifty years. In April 1997, Baseball Commissioner Bud Selig retired Robinson's number, 42, in perpetuity and established April 15 as Jackie Robinson Day, declaring that his debut in 1947 was "baseball's proudest and its most powerful social statement." In 2009, all major league players and coaches started the practice of wearing number 42 in games on April 15.

Jack Roosevelt Robinson was born in Cairo, Georgia, on January 31, 1914, the youngest of five raised in relative poverty by a single mother. As an infant, he was taken to Pasadena, California, where he was an outstanding athlete in high school, in junior college, and at UCLA, excelling in football, basketball, and track, as well as baseball. He withdrew from the university in his third year to help his mother. During the Second World War, he served a couple of years in the army and then played baseball for the Kansas City Monarchs in the Negro League. It was there that Jackie attracted the attention of Branch Rickey, the president and general manager of the Brooklyn Dodgers, who, for both moral and financial reasons, was looking for the right person to integrate baseball, a player who had not only great baseball skills but also the solid character needed to withstand the intense and inevitable racial harassment.

Convinced Robinson was his man, Rickey signed him to play a year in the minors with the intention of bringing him to the majors in 1947. When the Dodger players realized Rickey intended to play Robinson, some of them circulated a petition telling their boss that they would not play with him. When Pee Wee Reese, the Dodger's star shortstop, refused to sign the petition, however, the other players withdrew it. Reese grew up in Kentucky, where he went to high school in Louisville and played for the Louisville Colonels until he was signed in 1939 by the Brooklyn Dodgers. Though raised in the segregated South, Reese did not inherit explicit racial prejudices, thanks to his open-minded father. He went out of his way to befriend Jackie and to defend him against the vicious racial attacks by fans and other teams. The story is told that on May 13, 1947, the Dodgers were playing the Reds in Cincinnati and, in the first inning, the fans were giving Robinson such a hard time that Pee Wee came over from shortstop and put his arm around Jackie, silencing the crowd. There are questions about the accuracy of the story, but it has become an iconic moment in the history of baseball, a "historical symbol of friendship, teamwork and courage," as Jackie's widow, Rachel Robinson, stated at the 2005 unveiling of a statue commemorating the event.

All his life Robinson worked for civil rights and racial justice. While serving as a twenty-five-year-old army lieutenant at Fort Hood, Texas, he refused to move to the back of a segregated bus, which led to his arrest and court martial. Fortunately, he was found not guilty and given an honorable discharge. Robinson saw his illustrious baseball career—a lifetime batting average of .311, awards as Rookie of the Year and MVP, a World Series victory, and induction into the Hall of Fame in 1962—as furthering the cause of racial equality. After retiring from baseball, he got involved in business activities that helped improve the housing situation for minorities. He was an active member of the NAACP and a prolific fundraiser. He consistently pushed baseball to hire more Black executives and managers. In his autobiography, *I Never Had It Made*, published shortly before his death from a heart attack on October 24, 1972, at age fifty-three, Jackie Robinson wrote, "I cannot possibly believe that I have it made while so many black brothers and sisters are hungry, inadequately housed, insufficiently clothed, denied their dignity as they live in slums or barely exist on welfare." Words worthy of critical reflection today, a half century later.

*How can Jackie Robinson's life story inspire a continuing effort to overcome racial prejudice in our country?*

# MARTIN LUTHER KING JR. (1929–1968)

The enduring legacy of Dr. Martin Luther King Jr. helps us see the world and hear the Christian message from the perspective of the dispossessed and the powerless. While he himself grew up in middle-class economic conditions and enjoyed the advantages of higher education, he did experience striking instances of racial prejudice, which enabled him to achieve genuine empathy for the oppressed. He gave voice to the unheard cries of the poor and helped put the cruel face of oppression on our TV screens. His preaching showed how biblical themes and images could be used as a catalyst for action on behalf of justice, rather than as an opiate to create passive dependency.

Those of us who enjoy status and privilege in our society can never fully appreciate what it means to be powerless and faceless, but the life of Dr. King, with its powerful combination of insightful analysis and practical action, can remind us of our own privilege and direct our attention to the plight of those who are marginalized. His charismatic leadership of the nonviolent civil rights movement forced many citizens to confront the injustice in our society. His example moved us to a greater empathy for the oppressed. He called for "nonviolent gadflies to create the kind of tension in society that will help men rise from the dark depths of prejudice to see the majestic heights of understanding and brotherhood." He continues to be such a gadfly for us today.

From the beginning of his ministry as a pastor in Montgomery, Alabama, Dr. King argued brilliantly for racial justice by combining our national ideals and fundamental Christian teaching. If our cause is wrong, he contended, then the Constitution is wrong, and Jesus was nothing but a utopian dreamer. Dr. King did indeed criticize both the nation and the church for not living up to their ideals, but, at the same time, he drew on their resources and symbols in the struggle for human liberation. He asked how we as a nation could tolerate millions of poor people in our affluent country and castigated the Christian churches for their silence in the face of human suffering and for their tacit support of unjust social and economic systems. At the same time, he demanded that America live out the true meaning of its creed that all people are created equal and challenged the churches to follow the example of Jesus who came to liberate captives and preach the good news to the poor.

Dr. King wanted social change and realized that this required the mobilization of the best of our common traditions. Articulating the inspiring dream of all God's children living in peace and harmony, King said, "To produce change, people must be organized to work together in units of power." King envisioned an inclusive beloved community where all God's children, diverse as they are, would come together in a common cause to create a more just and peaceful world.

In our troubled world today, we need the prophetic witness of Dr. King more than ever. We need his respect for civil discourse in our culture so prone to harsh rhetoric; his commitment to nonviolence in our society threatened by random violence; his belief in human equality in our country still crippled by systemic racism; his call to action addressed to the Christian community tempted to apathy and complacency; his dedication to expanding solidarity in our deeply divided world; and finally, his steadfast and effective Christian witness to encourage us to maintain hope.

*How can our society be more faithful to the memory of Dr. King?*

# JOHN LEWIS (1940–2020)

The civil rights icon and seventeen-term U.S. Representative John Lewis, who was born February 21, 1940, the third of ten children in a sharecropper family, died on July 17, 2020, at the age of eighty. He was honored with a public funeral carried on national television that included eulogies by three former presidents: Bill Clinton, George W. Bush, and Barack Obama.

When John was fifteen, he heard a radio talk by Martin Luther King Jr. advocating the philosophy of nonviolence and insisting that there is a moral obligation to speak out against injustice and to help build the Beloved Community. When he met Dr. King in person, three years later, John knew that "he could not turn back" on his nonviolent quest for justice.

Interested in church ministry, John attended the American Baptist Theological Seminary in Nashville and, after completing his studies, was ordained a Baptist minister. He went on to earn a bachelor's degree in religion and philosophy from Fisk University.

During his collegiate years, he attended workshops taught by scholar and activist James Lawson, who urged young people to learn and practice the philosophy of nonviolence advocated by Gandhi as an effective means to achieve social change. John came to see nonviolence as "the way of peace, the way of love, as a way of living, not just a technique," which guided and inspired him throughout his life.[3]

John started his activist career by participating in a series of sit-ins, which exposed him to angry whites and landed him in jail but succeeded in desegregating lunch counters in downtown Nashville. In the early 1960s, Lewis helped organize a group of thirteen Freedom Riders—six whites and seven Blacks—who traveled by bus from Washington, DC, to New Orleans to challenge state laws, which prohibited Blacks and whites from sitting together on public transportation. Despite being assaulted, beaten, and jailed, Lewis and his companions persisted in their quest for racial justice through nonviolent protests.

On March 7, 1965, Lewis helped lead over six hundred marchers across the Edmund Pettus Bridge in Selma, where they were met by Alabama State Troopers who ordered them to disperse. When the protesters knelt in prayer, the mounted troopers charged and beat them. On that "Bloody Sunday," Lewis received a blow to the head that fractured his skull and sent him to the hospital but did not break his spirit or deter him from later completing the march to Montgomery.

Unlike his heroes, Martin Luther King Jr. and Robert Kennedy, who died at a young age, John Lewis carried on his commitment to civil rights into old age, serving over three decades in Congress. Over time, his moral integrity won him the respect of his colleagues, who recognized him as the "conscience of

---

3. See "Fall 1958—Nonviolence Studies," https://www.johnandlillianmileslewis foundation.org/the-lewis-legacy-working/.

Congress."[4] His commitment to nonviolence influenced some of his positions: for example, opposing the Iraq War and leading a sit-in on the floor of the House urging the passage of gun-control legislation.

As he was dying, John Lewis wrote an essay to be published on the day of his "homegoing" service—a final call to action applicable to all of us. After experiencing the Black Lives Matter movement, Lewis was encouraged that "the truth is still marching on." He expressed hope that historians of the twenty-first century will say that today's activists "laid down the heavy burdens of hate at last and that peace finally triumphed over violence, aggression and war." Furthermore, he insisted that ordinary people "can redeem the soul of America" by "participating in the democratic process" and by getting into "good trouble, necessary trouble," that is, constructive action on behalf of justice and peace. He urged them to "answer the highest calling of your heart" and follow the "more excellent way," "the way of peace, the way of love and nonviolence." The last inspiring words of John Lewis can speak to all of us: "So I say to you, walk with the wind, brothers and sisters, and let the spirit of peace and the power of everlasting love be your guide."[5]

*Is there any "good trouble" we should embrace to further the cause of civil rights and racial justice?*

# JOHN COURTNEY MURRAY (1904–1967)

As we look for ways to overcome the partisan polarization that continues to undermine our democratic process, we can

4. Renée Graham, "John Lewis—the 'Conscience of Congress,' the Conscience of America," *Boston Globe*, July 18, 2020, www.bostonglobe.com.

5. John Lewis, "Together, You Can Redeem the Soul of Our Nation," Opinion, *New York Times*, July 17, 2020, www.nytimes.com.

find wise guidance in the work of John Courtney Murray, SJ, the most influential Catholic theologian in the history of the United States. In his book *We Hold These Truths*, originally published during the presidential campaign in 1960, Murray recognized the threats to our democracy posed by "modern day barbarians" who resort to force and fear and who "replace dialogue with mono-logue, reason with passion and civility with harsh rhetoric."[6] He identified "structures of passion and war," which include hidden resentments and profound distrust among citizens and elected officials that threaten to turn healthy pluralism into destructive polarization. Rejecting the utopian notion of achieving unity among disparate worldviews, he proposed the more realistic goal of understanding the diverse viewpoints operative in our politi-cal process. Practically, we should strive to limit the warfare and enlarge the dialogue.

Murray insisted that constructive argument among responsible citizens is the great tool for deepening national self-understanding and creating a society of justice, peace, and unity. The health of the country depends on informed citizens debat-ing the proper response of government to the problems of public order, as well as the best ways of achieving the broader societal goal of furthering the common good. Such conversations require not only mutual trust but also a common language, initial points of agreement, and a core of commonly held truths. We can argue constructively only within a context of fundamental agreement.

Americans share an "emotional solidarity" because we inhabit a rich and vast land, share a common history of building a new nation, and are committed to the free pursuit of happiness. Furthermore, we share a common public philosophy based on self-evident truths known by reason: all persons are created equal, pos-sess a sacred personal dignity, and have certain inalienable rights.

---

6. John Courtney Murray, *We Hold These Truths: Catholic Reflections on the American Proposition* (New York: Rowman & Littlefield, 2005).

We honor justice as the goal and ground of civil law and believe in the "principle of consent" by which we accept the rule of law as the basis for social stability and orderly change. Given this common ground, Murray envisions concerned citizens "locked together in argument" and passionately engaged in serious discussion about significant public policy issues. The political task is to achieve enough common ground so that we can have a genuine argument about issues, which is possible only if we respect truth and hold significant shared truths.

What Murray wrote sixty years ago is still relevant today. We need a conscious decision to move beyond the wounds and prejudices that have accumulated over the years among persons with competing worldviews and political viewpoints. Furthermore, we must recognize that civil discourse is in the best interests of all citizens and that cooperative effort, based on mutual understanding and trust, is our best hope of improving our society. Dialogue must be enlarged because the great political and social questions have, in Murray's phrase, "a growing edge." This means that questions are not solved once and for all by simplistic measures proposed by one of the competing interest groups. Rather, they demand continuing dialogue among all segments of society to reach provisional solutions in changing circumstances.

*How can John Courtney Murray help us transform political polarization into a healthy pluralism?*

# Postscript

As we develop a distinctive American spirituality for our changing world, we do well to consider the broad perspectives provided by Pope Francis. In a series of interviews and talks given in 2021, Francis referenced the COVID-19 pandemic, which touched all of us by "invading our thoughts and attacking our dreams and plans." This means "today no one can afford to rest easy. The world will never be the same again." Nevertheless, the pandemic, which functioned like "an alarm signal," contained "signs which may prove to be the cornerstones of reconstruction," providing opportunities for "wise and far-sighted choices for the good of humanity."[1]

For Francis, building a better world requires the virtue of solidarity, which provides a broad vision of our immense world as a "global village," where "everything is interconnected" and where everyone works together for the universal common good. Solidarity also calls for cooperative local efforts, grassroots initiatives and

---

1. Junno Arocho Esteves, "Post-pandemic World Must Learn from Mistakes, Pope Says," *National Catholic Reporter*, May 15, 2021, www.ncronline.org. See also Pope Francis, *God and the World to Come* (Vatican City: Vatican Publishing House, 2021).

synodal approaches to Church engagement in building a better world.

The pope envisions a world where the old "normality of injustice, inequality and environmental degradation" is replaced by the "normality of the kingdom" where there is "enough bread" for everyone and "social organization is based on contributing, sharing and distributing, not on possessing, excluding and accumulating." A more equitable distribution of resources does not mean "depriving people who are better off" but does mean making sure the rights of marginalized people are respected. Francis gives special attention to caring for our earth and developing sustainable energy resources. He calls us to work together for a variety of causes: eradicating "bullying, poverty and corruption" as well as providing health care for all, equal opportunities for women, and hope for young people. In a viable post-pandemic world, nations will cooperate in solving common problems, such as preventing wars, limiting the arms race, and controlling global warming. The world must be "fraternally united" against "short-sighted nationalism, propaganda, isolationism and other forms of political selfishness."

Pope Francis has an urgent message for the whole human family. We all have a responsibility to share in the great task of building a better world from the "rubble" created by the COVID-19 crisis. He insists that "there is something worse than this crisis: the drama of wasting it" by "closing in on ourselves." We all must do our own part, "without delegating or passing the buck," to fight injustice and build "a new world order." In meeting our responsibilities, Pope Francis encourages us to rely on prayer and to trust Christ, who came to heal both the physical and social ailments that plague the world and who gave us the "necessary gifts to love and heal as he did, in order to take care of everyone without distinction of race, language, or nation."

Francis reminds us that we are part of a global rebuilding movement, which requires international cooperation and distinctive approaches in each country. We must work together and form coalitions to promote progress at the local level. We should insist that the Church has a right and an obligation to participate in the great task of building a better world, working through its institutional forms, and utilizing the gifts of its members. We should remember that the Catholic tradition has valuable resources for creating a more humane and just world, including, for example, the scriptures, the sacraments, the fathers and doctors of the Church, great theologians and mystics, conciliar and papal teaching, charitable institutions, and modern social teaching. Finally, Pope Francis encourages us to pray to Christ for guidance and follow his example in doing our part to develop a contemporary spirituality that promotes the "normalcy" of the kingdom of justice, peace, and love.